FOR WHATEVER IT'S WORTH:
IT'S NEVER TOO LATE TO BE
WHOEVER YOU WANT TO BE.

I HOPE YOU LIVE A LIFE
YOU'RE PROUD OF,

AND IF YOU FIND THAT
YOU'RE NOT,

I HOPE YOU HAVE THE
STRENGTH TO START OVER.

F. Scott Fitzgerald

First printing 2020

ISBN 978-1-71659-592-9

This book is dedicated to my wife Rose, and my immediate family, who put up with my nonsense for years. Love you!

Unfinished Business is a non-fiction publication. Details have been described as accurately as possible but are not guaranteed as such, as the author did his best to recollect events as they occurred. But hey, he is getting old, so give him a break. *No part of this work can be reproduced or transmitted in any form without the express written permission of the copyright owner.*

To contact the Author & Publisher, information is below:

Nate Cross
24641 Framingham Drive
Westlake, OH 44145
Email: **cross.nate@yahoo.com**

Let me know what you think. Feel free to email me with comments, and/or let me know if I can ever be of help to you!

IN MEMORIAM

For My Father: This is the book my Dad, *James Cross*, never wrote. He passed away in 2014. For years, he told my many brothers and sister that he was "working on a book" that never got written. Oddly, I too found myself sharing that same aspiration with my children. As a result, I vowed I would someday write a book. This is that book.

James Cross was one of Cleveland's most famous hairstylists as a result of his work at all of the *Halle Department Store Beauty Salons,* where he developed a strong client-base of Cleveland's most prominent "movers and shakers" subsequent to his move from his birthplace of Toronto, Canada to Cleveland, in 1964. However, his greatest achievement was his role as husband and father, as reflected by the many stories and jokes he shared with his nine children, which we all can recite word for word, always eliciting a laugh. *He lives on in each of us.*

For My Brother: Sadly, my brother *John Paul Cross* passed away from cancer in March of 2020. He was only 40 years old. Upon his death, my desire to finish the Great Divide, to memorialize his life, became an obsession. On many occasions during my ride, I felt his presence. He was not only with me in spirit, but lives on through every good deed I am blessed to be able to carry forward for others, which in my mind is the ultimate tribute I can pay to him, as that's the type of person he was.

***All proceeds from this book
benefit the mission of *2 CIR-CLE RACING*
to help those struggling with addictions.***

Our logo says a lot about us.

It shows what we hope to achieve: to use the two circles of our bicycle wheels to help move people from the chaos of addiction (right wheel) to a more ordered path of recovery (left wheel). *The name itself is an acronym:* **CIR** *(Community-In-Recovery)* **CLE** *(Cleveland).*

So, who are we?

We are a team of experienced cyclists who are as passionate about addiction recovery as we are about racing bikes. In one way or another, each of us associated with this team has been touched by the disease of substance abuse disorder. Our goals are simple: use our relationships, resources and visibility as riders to help ***erase the stigma of addiction*** and ***help provide resources to people struggling with addictions*** as well as the families and loved ones of those struggling alongside them.

How can we help?

Often, the hardest part of recovery is knowing where to start. Visit our website to learn more and find links to available resources such as treatment programs, peer support, sober living facilities, meetings and therapists. Substance abuse disorders impact more than just individuals. We also provide resources aimed at providing support and healing for families and loved ones.

Community Involvement: We participate in local community events to demonstrate that there is nothing stigmatic about this disease. We also partner with local organizations that provide resources to those currently in or seeking recovery to supplement their programming. This includes lifestyle, job opportunities and outreach. Additionally, this also includes an effort to obtain and fix-up donated bikes to be given to those in recovery, so they can utilize their bike as a "vehicle" toward recovery. We also offer group rides to those struggling with addictions.

To learn more, visit:

www.2circleracing.org

The Great Divide Route

The Course: Banff (Alberta), Canada to the Mexico Border

Total Distance: 2,745 miles

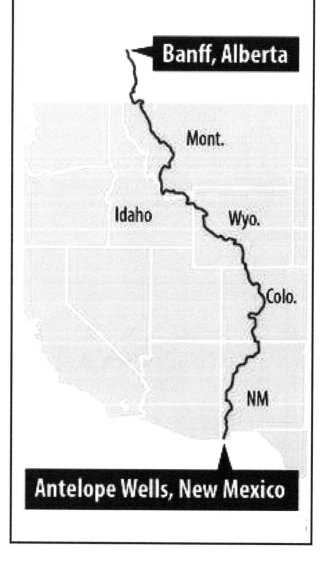

The **BEST** view comes after the **HARDEST** climb

"What lies behind us and what lies before us are tiny matters compared to what lies within us."

Ralph Waldo Emerson

TABLE OF CONTENTS

AUTHOR'S NOTE:

Pastor Konan Stephens is a remarkable person I met after watching <u>youtube</u> videos chronicling his journey in the 2016 Tour Divide. After viewing his videos, which really helped me prepare for my 2019 Tour Divide race, I realized that Konan lived in Columbus, Ohio. I called Konan and asked if we could meet so I could "pick his brain" about his experience on this ride. He was gracious with his time and became someone I began to truly admire, especially because his spiritual and motivational messages resonated with me.

Aside from being an inspirational leader, Konan is also an incredible athlete. With no real cycling or mountain biking experience, Konan bought an inexpensive bike and rode in the 2016 Tour Divide, having completed the route in 22 days/11 hours -- finishing in 30th place out of 198 starters. He is also no stranger to other unique challenges, as he has climbed Mt. Kilimanjaro; participated in 100-mile endurance races; and has completed the Rim-to-Rim-to-Rim Grand Canyon Run, to name a few of his crazy adventures.

He is also no stranger to the cause of addiction, as he rode in the 2016 Tour Divide to raise funds and bring awareness to Tyler's Light, a non-profit drug abuse prevention and awareness organization near his hometown in the Columbus, OH area. He is an inspirational leader and pastor, and a person I admire and respect. I hope you enjoy his Foreward.

"Unfinished Business"

FOREWARD

By Konan Stephens
Pastor, C3 Church

I can still remember connecting with Nate over lunch on that Sunday afternoon. He had the fire burning in his heart to do this crazy adventure called the "Tour Divide." It's the kind that once it gets lodged in your heart, you just can't shake it. I know it well because that was my story a couple years earlier.

I'm a believer that we are shaped by our experiences. They stretch us, challenge us and push us up or pull us down. We can't choose all the experiences we face in life. Sometimes we are thrown into a situation or something outside our control that explodes around us, hitting us with shrapnel. Other experiences we choose. Everything from the family trip to Disney to taking on a new hobby, they all shape us.

So, what could happen if we began to intentionally go after experiences that we knew would shape us for the better? We could choose the experiences that could shape us into the person we would like to be. This journey from Canada to Mexico will shape all those who dare try to take it on. I've personally experienced that, and this book allows you to see it through Nate's eyes. As I turned the pages of this book, I found myself reliving the memories and the emotions all over again. It is a roller coaster of a ride, so strap in and get ready.

Unfinished Business is a story of redemption. Redemption is very seldom an easy road, but one of wrestling and struggle. Much like the transformation of the butterfly, the struggle can produce beauty if handled correctly. Nate's transparency through his struggle is refreshing and it challenges us to examine our own lives to take steps forward.

Honestly, we all have issues, struggles and battles we fight that others may not see. Most of us, if we are honest, wear masks that hide our own brokenness, fears, insecurities and issues. While some may be better at hiding them than others, we can only hide them for so long. In this life, we are all running *FROM something or TO something*. Until we answer the deeper questions of "what?" and "why?" we will continue to struggle with the same issues. For many, we never define our enemy and an enemy undefined is an enemy undefeated. This story is one of finally owning up to what had owned him. Nate chose to run at his addiction. He made a decision and then made good on his decision.

My personal opinion is: two of the greatest gifts in this life are relationships and experiences. Both of them shape us. It's been said, "Experience is the greatest teacher." I don't believe that to be true. Evaluated experience is the greatest teacher. As Nate relives his journey, he takes us with him. His highs and lows and the lessons he learned along the way are applicable to our lives. It could even be said that the way it all worked out for him causes him to even appreciate it more.

Every day is a gift. That's why we call it the present. When our lives are over, we will ask ourselves if we really lived it to the fullest. There was a study done where they asked people in their 80's if they could live their lives over again, what would they have done differently? One of the top answers was, *"They would have risked more."* The way I look at it, the fruit is always out on the limb and you have to go out on the limb to get it. Nate did something very bold by going public with this BHAG (Big Hairy Audacious Goal). When we do this, it is a huge risk. Because we are then haunted by the questions, "What if?" "What if I fail?" "What if I quit?" "What if I get hurt?" "What if?" "What if?" "What if?" To that I say, "SO WHAT!" So what if I fail? Failure does not define me. So what if I'm forced to quit? I can always try again. So what if I get hurt? I'll use the experience to make me stronger. SO WHAT!

The truth is, each one of us is either under our past and buried by it, or we stand on top of it and are able to reach higher. _Unfinished Business_ is a story that most of us can relate with. One of ups and downs, of defeat and triumph and of never giving up. Honestly, the only time we lose is when we give up for good.

Plans in life very rarely go exactly as planned. Life is all about navigating through difficulties and problems. For those who don't get back up and keep trying, they will miss out on so much. Mike Tyson once said, "Everyone has a plan until they get punched in the face." This is a story of how to get back up after being knocked down.

Think about the story of your life. With each decision and every day that passes, you are writing the story of your life. What story will those closest to you tell about you? Never forget that the pen is in your hand, so make the most of it!

As I read the chapters of this book, I relived much of my own journey on a bike across the wilderness from Canada to Mexico. This ride is life changing. It stays with you forever. There is not a week that goes by where I don't reflect about what it did inside of me. I believe that shared experiences have a way of uniting us. There is something powerful that happens when people overcome the same or similar obstacles. It's a strong connection. It's similar to the end of "The Lord of the Rings" where Frodo, Sam, Merry and Pippen, having just had the adventure of a lifetime, are sitting in the pub having a drink. Everyone around them was dancing and singing with no understanding of what they just encountered. Yet those four hobbits were changed. As they looked into each other's eyes, no words had to be said, because they just knew. The battles they fought, the pain they endured and the adventure they experienced, would change their lives forever. There would forever be a bond that would unite them as brothers, and I now feel this same connection with Nate Cross.

May this book challenge you to reach higher and fight harder than ever before. Nate has fought and will continue to fight his battles. There are new challenges and higher heights that are yet to be reached, not only for Nate, but also for you. Don't sit back. Don't be passive, for passivity leads to captivity. Nate was willing to stare his fears in the eye. He took action and never gave up. There is nothing stopping you, but you. Live a life with no regrets. Every new day creates new opportunities for those gutsy enough to step out into the unknown. So, take action today and GO LIVE YOUR ADVENTURE!

14

PROLOGUE

Life's Challenge

"You can't go back and change the beginning, but you can start where you are and change the ending."

C.S. Lewis

This is a story about my adventure while completing the Great Divide Mountain Bike Trail, a 2,745-mile mountain bike route from Banff (Alberta, Canada) to the border of the United States and Mexico (Antelope Wells, New Mexico), on and along the Great Divide (also known as the Continental Divide).

However, this book is much more than that, as it is a reflective story about a life changing event. I also share some personal reflections on events that have occurred in my life that provide the source of my inspiration, while attempting to complete the Great Divide, on my mountain bike.

Although my ride concluded on June 2, 2020, my journey truly began while in college, during the years 1982-1989, while a student at Cleveland State University, as I pursued my Bachelor of Arts (Communication); and subsequently my Master of Public Administration Degree (MPA). During this point in my life, I not only discovered my love for drinking (mostly beer), but also put myself on a destructive path of eventual and continued life-long abuse of alcohol.

For me, I never considered myself an alcoholic, but instead referred to myself as someone who just loved to drink. My drinking was never a daily occurrence, but rather, a weekend hobby or habit that never stopped. In fact, when people accused me of being an alcoholic early in my life, I would usually respond with my standard joke: "What's the difference between a drunk and an alcoholic?" followed by my usual punchline: "Drunks don't have to go to all those damn meetings!" I would then make an emphatic point I had *no need for meetings*.

This standard punchline, and joke, illustrated my feeling toward my drinking. In my mind, I was never an alcoholic, or so I thought. I just liked to drink, or so I told myself. As I reflect now, indeed, I am an alcoholic. I always was. I still am, and I always will be. I just never knew what it meant.

I also certainly never understood the damage, consequences or impact my drinking had on me, or others close to or important to me. Today that is not the case, as I have come to terms with who I am as an alcoholic, which I never fully understood. Nor did I know much about the disease throughout my entire adult life, until I quit drinking on November 22, 2016. *This was a day I will never forget.* And while it is sad it took me over 35+ years to come to terms with my self-diagnosis, and most importantly a personal decision to quit drinking, I hurt many people along the way.

That is the purpose of this book: to put my past into perspective, and to share the parallels that have occurred during my recovery and during this ride on the Great Divide, *as I have found cycling to be the perfect "vehicle" for my recovery.*

But before I share my adventure, it is appropriate and necessary to put my drinking into perspective, as everything I did throughout my adult life involved drinking. Sure, I was mostly a "weekend drunk" but the fact of the matter is, I never knew when to stop. I was a "binge drinker" who wanted nothing more than to "get trashed" as I loved to get drunk. That is why I drank, or so I thought. However, as I have learned throughout my recovery process, since becoming an active member of Alcoholics Anonymous (AA), there is much more to this story than just my desire to get drunk. I have come to realize that I was powerless over alcohol; I just never could stop drinking once I started.

As I look back on my distant past, it is ironic that one of my first experiences with alcohol involved dumping hundreds upon hundreds of cases of beer, per week, down the drain. This was during a period when I was 12-14 years old, as I had one of the oddest jobs a teenager could ever have. It was during a time when kids my age collected beer cans, and at one point, I had a beer can collection of over 500+ different types of beer cans. During this time, at a local beer can show, I met a man by the name of Richard Balog, from Shaker Heights, OH.

Richard had a nice little business, as he figured out that empty beer cans, with the top of the can intact so as to protect the integrity of the can (to ensure their value for collectors like me) were more valuable empty rather than full. Problem was, he needed the cans emptied so he could ship these empty cans all around the country, to collectors like me that were willing to pay $1.00 for each type of beer can to enhance their collection. He would then sell a can for a minimum of $1-buck per can. Thus, a case he bought for $8 would now be worth triple, so long as it was empty. That is where I came in.

Richard would pay me 20-cents per case to empty and dump beer down the drain, which translated to approximately $8.00 to $10.00 per hour, given my eventual efficiency, which was not bad for a teenager looking for a part-time job. As a result of this odd part-time vocation, my family enjoyed the fruits of this labor, as they got to drink all kinds of beer, from all around the world, for free -- so long as they were opened from the bottom.

Ironically, despite this odd introduction to alcohol, I never drank nor liked drinking, especially at that age. One would think that as an eventual alcoholic, the seeds could have been planted at this stage of my life. However, even as I grew older while in high school, I never really drank. My interests laid elsewhere as I used to run track and cross country and work other part-time jobs to pay my tuition for school. Though, once I graduated from high school and went to college and joined a fraternity, my desire to "drink and party" was not really any different from most kids my age who went to college. In my case though, as is everything in my life, I like to take things to the extreme. This is where my problem began.

In sum, once I entered college, I lived to drink. It probably did not help that I immediately moved into a fraternity house prior to my first fall classes, at the age of 18 (at that time, the legal drinking age). And while I figured I was "late to the game" in terms of not drinking in high school, it did not take long for me to make up for lost time. Within a short period of time, I became the "beverage manager" at our fraternity and was soon lining up 10-15 kegs of beer every Friday for each weekend's party, events which were steady and consistent. I also was given the keys to a "pop machine" which we diligently stocked solely with cheap beer, which could be bought for 30-cents per can. With the keys to the machine, and a fund to stay stocked, I had an endless supply of inventory. That was never lost on me either, as I felt like I had the keys to the kingdom.

This was only the beginning, and I could go on and on about endless parties and opportunities to drink. Suffice it to say, I took advantage of every opportunity, throughout my undergraduate and post-graduate years, which became the foundation for my habit, that eventually lead to a lifestyle of weekend drinking. And when I drank, I was never a responsible drinker who knew when to stop, but instead became a binge drinker, always focused on one goal: to get hammered.

Within time, my life changed professionally upon graduation, but my "partying ways" never did. All the years through my twenties, thirties & forties -- seldom was there a weekend or "special occasion" (which became more frequent and less "special") in which I was not drinking. One thing that never changed though, was my conviction that I was never an alcoholic. In that context, I considered myself to be a responsible drinker who never allowed drinking to get in the way of my professional functions, which became important to me as I became involved in charitable and political causes (see Appendix 1).

The bottom line, despite my view otherwise, I became a functioning alcoholic, as my partying ways never really changed after college, including the weekend binges. Whether it was a social engagement, sporting event or an excuse like yardwork -- I was always willing and able to find some rationale whereby I deserved the opportunity to get drunk. All of this was in line with my attitude of "work hard, play hard."

Thus, I lived my life on two parallel paths. On one hand, I acted in a professional manner whereby I was absolutely convinced of my self-control as someone who did all the right things, and made all the right moves. I also was always willing to help others through my chosen professional, charitable, political and civic roles, with the attitude and mindset that I was making a difference. Indeed, I did many things I was proud of. However, this was the professional Nate Cross.

From a personal standpoint, though, I also lived my life on another dual path, whereby I continued my weekend partying. Beer was my weapon on this careless ride. Specifically, I continued to find every excuse under the sun to celebrate any personal achievement, while also beginning to raise a family. While doing so, I also found every excuse to continue to drink as a reward for my personal achievements as well. This became the foundation of my every single social interaction, with anyone, all within a hard-partying social circle.

In sum, drinking became who I was, always with the justification that so long as I continued to function both personally and professionally, who was I hurting anyway? Indeed, I created a trail of damage along the way.

My personally destructive behavior is best illustrated by my first serious legal offense, when I got pulled over for a DUI (driving under the influence) after watching an NFL football playoff game in the Cleveland Flats (a social entertainment district of Cleveland). I was 33-years-old at the time. This incident was not just another frivolous college incident, as I had convinced myself to believe for decades, but rather, an inevitable outcome destined to occur as I would often drink all day, then foolishly decide to drive, which became a recurring pattern.

Aside from the legal consequences, it was a costly mistake as I had to hire a lawyer to represent me in court. This was humiliating and humbling, to say the least. I also did everything I could to make sure this did not impact my professional life. Thus, I tried to hide this incident from everyone (including my family) and most important at the time, my potential future employer, as I was near the tail-end of the interviewing process for a job as the Executive Director of a national non-profit healthcare organization. This was a position I wanted desperately and knew if the news of this incident found its way into the interview process, I would not land the job. Somehow, I was miraculously able to avoid having to share this information (I was never asked) and landed the position. Problem solved, or so I thought.

I also vowed that I would not "drink and drive" ever again. For a good 10-years, this goal was achieved. Ironically though, my drinking and the same weekend drinking pattern continued, as I figured my big mistake was the "driving" after having a few beers, and certainly not the actual act of drinking. That is what an alcoholic does, we rationalize everything. And for me, that meant everything. Everything.

In my mind, so long as I was able to avoid putting myself into the situation of not driving after having a few beers, it was "full steam ahead" to carry on with my weekend drinking. This was the pattern that escalated over the course of the next 19-years. During that time, I carried on as if I was still in college, despite the fact that I had a good "ten-year run" of never actually driving after I had been drinking. This rationalization became my way of saying to others: "You see, I don't have a drinking problem, nor am I an alcoholic."

This mindset, especially knowing I would not be driving during my weekend exploits, allowed me to further rationalize that I could get even more hammered, especially when I had my ride all worked out. Of course, this never had an impact on me, as I relied on others to drive me all around town, at all hours of the day and night. This responsibility became especially hard on my wife Rose, most of all, as she became my designated driver, for decades. She also had to put up with "Drunk Boy" (as she would cleverly and deservedly call me). As the years wore on, this whole pattern continued. But it also got worse, as my disease progressed, as it does for most alcoholics.

Within time, after a decade of having a personal "zero tolerance" attitude about "drinking and driving," I slowly but surely began to get back behind the wheel, after a few beers. This is typical for people like me, who do everything to the extreme; I rationalized that this is not only okay, but also that I was a good driver while drunk! Incredible!?

Others noticed my behavior and were increasingly concerned. I just never wanted to hear about it. I reflect back on one episode in which my very good friend Nab, a tough Vietnam Veteran who has *seen it all,* once pulled me aside and told me that some of our other close friends (Jeff, Jack, Gary and Larry) were very concerned about my drinking, and some of the poor decisions I was making. Of course, I scoffed at the notion that I had a problem, but that conversation did resonate with me. Unfortunately, I just never did anything about it. I also always viewed my behavior as "pretty normal."

Indeed, my behavior was anything but normal. This point is reinforced by a conversation I remember overhearing when I was at the Leadville Mountain Bike Race in 2015, when I was with my good friend Rob (whom I rode with in Colorado, and you will read more about in subsequent chapters) and my other good friend, Dave. They had just returned from a bar, after two beers. I remember overhearing their conversation about our drinking days back in college. As they were reminiscing, I distinctly remember hearing them talk about how they do not ever recall a time, in the past decade, in which they ever got trashed. I was blown away by this, and puzzled, for several reasons.

First, I could never imagine having just two beers and leaving a bar, without drinking myself into oblivion, as I just never had any self-control to say: "Enough is enough." Secondly, having just gotten hammered the weekend before (and more-or-less every weekend since college), I could never imagine a scenario in which I would or could drink responsibly. You see, they are responsible drinkers, who enjoy an occasional beer, and this was foreign to me, and incomprehensible. I just never was a responsible drinker, as alcoholics like me are powerless over alcohol.

These types of encounters indeed had an impact on me, but I continued my pattern of recklessness, regardless. I also began to "master" the art of living my life on a dual path, and saw nothing wrong with partying hard, so long as I stayed out of trouble. For me, it was just a matter of time, and as you would surmise, would not take long for my behavior to catch up with me again as it did on the late afternoon of Saturday, November 22, 2016. This was the date of my last drink. This was also the date of my second DUI offense, in which I crashed my car into the back of another car, while that car was sitting innocently at a red light. *This was my wake-up call.* I was 52 years old.

Clearly, this was no longer some college mishap, as I was a grown adult who could have really hurt someone. Fortunately, the crash was just a fender-bender wherein no one got hurt, but it was a serious situation, nonetheless. This was also a blessing in disguise, as this was not only the day of my last drink, but an opportunity to put myself on a new path.

However, the consequences for this incident were significant. I now had to hire another lawyer, and was potentially facing jail time, given that it was my second DUI offense. As a result, I lost my ability to drive for 30-days, as I had refused a sobriety test. Additionally, I also had to deal with all the physical damage to my car and the crash victim's car, which fortunately (from a financial standpoint) my insurance covered, in addition to the possibility of not being able to drive to work, which was a privilege I certainly did not want to lose.

I could go on and on about all the shame and humiliation I had brought upon myself. But it was at this point I vowed to take my personal plight with absolute seriousness, as I was potentially facing a period of three to 90 days in jail. Additionally, I knew that by taking this seriously, it certainly would not hurt in the eyes of the judge, who would decide my fate during my sentencing hearing. And I took seriously every recommendation my lawyer suggested, including swiftly entering a 12-session alcohol assessment program, as I just wanted to move on from this humbling and embarrassing moment of my life.

Within the next month, I appeared in court for sentencing. By now, I had finally come to terms with the fact that I was guilty and needed to just deal with the consequences, as it was my actions which put me in this awful situation in the first place. *Again, to say this was the most embarrassing, humbling and lowest point in my life would be an understatement.* This was made even worse by the fact that I personally knew the judge, and knew her well, as she had sat as a member of my chapter board of trustees for the national non-profit organization in which I previously served as the Executive Director. I also respected this judge and knew anything less than total honesty with her would not only be disrespectful, but she would see right through it.

When the moment came for me to speak in court and plead guilty, my emotions got the best of me as I began to openly cry. I even remember the look on my lawyer's face, as he was caught by surprise, as I was truly and genuinely sobbing in court from my shame. Here I was, a grown man sobbing in open court. This was now not just the lowest point in my life (my "rock bottom") as a 52-year-old man, but knew I had a problem. *It was time to get honest with myself, and finally admit I had a serous drinking problem.*

Fortunately, in terms of the legal ramifications of this second DUI incident, the consequences were minimal, given what could have occurred. Ultimately, I was able to regain driving privileges (though for the next year, it was only to/from work), and there was no jail time. I was also ordered to pay all fines, received six-months of probation (and the occasional random "pee-test"), while also being ordered to continue my treatment in the assessment program, and attend meetings of Alcoholics Anonymous (AA) -- or else jail was imminent.

With vigor, I continued my treatment and attended meetings of Alcoholics Anonymous (in retrospect, this was one of the best things that has ever happened in my life), as I was now genuinely and sincerely determined to make something good come from this whole ordeal.

From the day I entered my assessment program, and meetings of Alcoholics Anonymous (AA), I was blown away by how ordinary and normal everyone else was in the program. I had clearly created an incorrect mental picture in my mind of what those in the room would look like (…of people on "skid-row"), but this was not the case. What I found interesting was how the room, occupied by people like me, were filled with both men and women who were from all walks of life: lawyers, doctors, housewives, students, bankers, construction workers, writers, restaurant employees, public servants, etc. This surprised me.

Concurrently, during the course of my 12-session treatment program, my progress evolved as I came to honestly assess that I was not just a "weekend partier" as I had come to convince myself, but rather, was in fact an alcoholic.

What sobriety taught me is that "the next drink" will put you right back where you started. That is why an alcoholic can never have "just one drink" as it is an immediate return to the destructive ways of the past, straight back to my "rock bottom" which for me is something that is not only unacceptable, but something I never ever want to relive.

This realization came from acknowledging that all my actions were in direct contradiction of the 12-Step Program, which are referenced more fully in the appendix of this book (Appendix 4) and most importantly, are part of my daily recovery.

And while you may think these 12-Steps are a checklist of "things one can do to combat" alcoholism, that is not necessarily the case, as the 12-Steps are more of a *mindset* of how to approach ones' life.

In this respect, the 12-Steps of Recovery are now incorporated daily into everything I do (including cycling, which I view as an essential element of my recovery) and who I am today, as my *mindset* has totally changed.

My new attitude is best reflected in a quote that was shared by my good friend Scott Evans, Founder of 2-CIR-CLE Racing, in a post on our cycling team's website:

"It is all about mindset. From the moment you wake up, to the moment you rest your head at night. Everything is up to you. Your emotions, your thoughts. Your perceptions, your reactions. Every moment."

This is the story of how the 12-Steps of Recovery helped me conquer the Great Divide, one day at a time.

Additionally, through cycling, this is also a story of personal redemption from my past, as a result of a new mindset I have been blessed with that has allowed me to enjoy the gift of *each day,* that God has given me, *one day at a time.*

INTRODUCTION

Ready To "Live My Adventure"

*"Whatever the mind can conceive,
and believe…it can achieve."*
Napoleon Hill

To this day, I still cannot quite figure out or recall how the idea to participate in a 2,745-mile self-supported mountain bike race, from Canada to Mexico, became an item on my bucket list.

However, once that seed was planted to participate in the 2019 Tour Divide (an annual self-supported race on the Great Divide route), I was determined to participate. I did everything I could to learn all about the race: I read every social media post; read every book available; watched every video about the ride; bought the best gear; trained hard; and was ready when I started the race. Though, nothing truly prepared me to grasp the full nature of my adventure.

Ultimately, my adventure took a longer time to complete than once initially thought, as I did indeed participate in the Tour Divide in 2019, but unfortunately *dropped out that year due to an illness on the ninth day of my race*, having completed close to 1,000 miles (with 80,000 feet of elevation gain!).

To say I was "bummed" that I dropped out of the 2019 Tour Divide would be an understatement. However, despite my disappointment, I was determined to return someday, to either compete again in the Tour Divide race, or to just non-competitively complete the Great Divide route. The following chapters chronicle both journeys: my 2019 Tour Divide race, and 2020 Great Divide ride.

Specifically, I will share the story and circumstances that led to that fateful day in June 2019 when I had to drop out of the 2019 Tour Divide race. I will then share and chronicle (one year later) the story of what it took to get back to the spot where I dropped out, after it was clear the 2020 Tour Divide race would not occur, due to a worldwide pandemic (Covid-19).

Thus, this is a story of two adventures: one that began in 2019 with the Tour Divide race; and another adventure that ended with my completion of the route almost one year later, in May of 2020, on my Great Divide ride.

However, my story would not be complete without putting the whole situation into context (leading up to my decision to ride the Great Divide in 2020), as who would have ever thought, at the beginning of 2020, that this would be the year of a worldwide pandemic, with the onset of Covid-19?

This pandemic clearly made the challenge of planning to compete in the Tour Divide race (in June of 2020) much more difficult, as it was not even clear in March if the race was even going to occur. Nor was it clear to anyone the impact Covid-19 would wreak upon the life of everyone worldwide.

As we know all too well, everyone across the entire globe was affected due to the outbreak of Covid-19. In the United States, statewide shelter-in-place orders were wreaking havoc with everyone's way of life; unemployment was skyrocketing; and most regrettably, lives were being lost. In this context, one would have thought that competing in this race would have been the furthest thing from my mind. Wrong.

Sadly, despite our whole way of life being changed, throughout the whole ordeal, I could not selfishly shed my obsession with participating in the 2020 Tour Divide race, to finish my Great Divide ride. I am a cyclist after all, and that is how we cyclists think. Sad indeed.

In retrospect, this mindset is truly pathetic, as this became my sole consuming thought, despite a worldwide pandemic. And while everyone, regardless of profession or location, had to endure incredible changes to their lives, and more horribly, people were dying and getting seriously ill from this unknown virus, here I was, thinking of nothing more than to figure out how I was going to get to the start line of a race. Again, this is how we cyclists think.

For me, this "new reality" began to really bum me out. I had trained long and hard through the winter months in Cleveland to prepare to race, and now all of my preparations started to wither away. In particular, as I began to search for information about whether or not the 2020 Tour Divide was to occur, I began to get angry that people were spreading disinformation via all social media platforms as to whether or not the 2020 Tour Divide would or should occur. I was also further bothered that everyone on social media seemed to become an overnight infectious disease expert, with the intent to dictate to me what I would or could not do. Clearly, a streak of anger and rebellion still exists within.

Ultimately, I just wanted to know if the race was going to happen, as races were getting cancelled week by week, well into the Summer of 2020. And while the Tour Divide is not an "official" race but rather an "organized unofficial gathering" and/or "annual challenge," information was nonetheless being circulated on social media platforms (*facebook* in particular) that seemed to doom the race, and this began to anger me.

To make matters worse, I also become further irritated that *public shaming* was occurring on all online social media platforms, as personal opinions began to dominate the discussion. This escalated to the point whereby people were being attacked online for the mere offense of having a differing point of view, relative to whether the race should occur. Subsequently, this online dialogue ultimately doomed my race plans (people were arguing that with the virus spreading, it would be foolish to do this race for fear of further spread of the virus, in towns along the route). Sure, they had a point, but many opposing views were shared too.

As an example, I shared an opinion that we should just wait until mid-May to see how the situation evolved, before cancelling the race, and wait until there was more accurate information or modeling. It was not long before someone would immediately hurl an online insult back at me with a personal attack, along with the suggestion that "any rider to cycle on the route in 2020 would not only be reckless, but selfish as well." I disagreed with this point of view, and made my case, as I viewed this cycling event as the ultimate social distance ride.

However, due to the onslaught of negativity on social media, the "Keyboard Coronavirus Cops" ultimately became the vocal online majority early in the Covid-19 epidemic and won the day. From the perspective of an obsessed cyclist wanting nothing more than to get to the starting line of a race, the practice of *social media shaming* spread fear among everyone, to the point where riders began to publicly express their misgivings about participating in the June race, and things snowballed from there. Granted, the Canadian border was temporarily closed, and there were some state border restrictions in place for a reason, as the pandemic was a serious situation. However, in my mind this did not take everything into account, and I felt that I could ride responsibly, despite the pandemic.

By the end of April of 2020, most people had assumed, and correctly so, that the Tour Divide race would not occur, with everyone being encouraged to just "wait until next year." It was at this point that I decided I would no longer engage in any further social media dialogue, as I knew in my heart that most people along the route would welcome visitors again, when restrictions were lifted.

My rationale for this belief was based on my premise that the areas we would cycle into were dependent on tourism, and people like me who came back into the area would be welcome as an economic "shot in the arm" to the economy. Indeed, that is exactly what happened.

Additionally, as is characteristic of me, I did not want to wait, nor did I want someone to tell me that I could not do something. And as much as I am a changed man in sobriety, some of my old traits (stubbornness and impatience) still exist.

Thus, I decided to stage my own personal protest by abandoning the whole concept of racing in the Tour Divide (which was "more or less" cancelled anyway) and instead just ride to complete the portion of the route I had not ridden in 2019. This decision warranted some reflection, as we were still in a worldwide pandemic, and I had some concerns.

If I continued with my plan to ride the Great Divide on the portions I had not completed, it would not be an easy ride. I still had three states to ride through (Wyoming, Colorado, and New Mexico), which represented over 1,700-miles with 80,000 additional feet of elevation gain climbing long mountain passes, which potentially could still be impassable due to snow, which often is the case in mid-May. I also had to deal with the scary thought that re-supply of food and water along the route might still be extremely difficult now, as some towns might still be in "lockdown" mode due to the pandemic.

Ultimately, my stubbornness and impatience won the day. I desperately wanted nothing more than to complete my Great Divide ride, as my decision to quit the race in 2019, due to an illness, still haunted me. I also had been going crazy from being in exile during my ten-week lockdown and was sick of being home. In my mind, this was the perfect time to go, as I had plenty of vacation time and this would be the ultimate "social distancing" ride. This would now become my "Freedom Ride" as I came to refer to it.

Subsequently, on May 4, 2020, I booked one of the few direct flights to the area near where I quit the previous year, with a solid plan to begin riding in mid-May. As my departure neared (with plans to fly into Denver, Colorado and rent a car to travel to my start point), I sent out a *facebook* post to announce my decision (with the subsequent photo):

> With Covid-19 affecting everyone's life, I could not think of a better time to take care of some "unfinished business" on the Great Divide Mountain Bike Route.
>
> As you may know, I participated in the Tour Divide last year, but "only" made it 1,000 miles in nine-days

(Banff, Canada; to an area near Yellowstone National Park in Wyoming), before getting sick and abandoning the effort. Since I "only have 1,700 miles to go" to reach the Mexico border (thru Wyoming, Colorado & New Mexico), I decided to head back to the "scene of the crime" and re-start where I left off.

My "Freedom Ride" (after 10 weeks of quarantine) should take 2-3 weeks, beginning sometime around May 15th. Aside from the challenge, I look forward to riding with my good friend Rob Andrew (and a few other cyclists on the Colorado portion of my ride), and plan to take some route diversions on some portions of the Great Divide trail, as some mountain passes are still "impassable" due to snow & mud. I also plan to take some breaks, enjoy myself along the way, and make sure I ride through towns that are open to re-supply with food & water! So, when and if you see me "off-route" that is by design, so I can be safe.

If you are interested to follow me on my self-supported "Freedom Ride" (as I socially distance from everyone), please just go to *trackleaders.com* and you should see my "dot" on the map to chart my progress.

Once and if I make it to the Mexican border, I'll likely share the news that I was able to take care of some "unfinished business" by completing my ride along the Great Divide Mountain Bike Route.

Again, it should take a few weeks. I then plan to visit my sister and mom, in Phoenix. Until then, happy trails!

Thus, after a defeat at the hands of the Tour Divide in 2019; the 2020 Tour Divide being cancelled; and a worldwide pandemic; I now had a plan -- it was Mexico or Bust!

CHAPTER ONE

2019 Tour Divide Race

Canada: Breathtaking & Beautiful

Banff (Alberta, Canada) to Montana (USA Border)
Approximately 267-miles (24,040 feet of elevation gain)

My adventure began with participation in the 2019 Tour Divide. At the time, this was just another race, purely for the sake of a challenge. I also had not yet made the connection between how my cycling could play a role in my recovery, as I was eventually able to discover and embrace. Also, I had only been in the AA program for two-years and was still working with my sponsor on my 12-Step Program.

However, the one common denominator in both the 2019 Tour Divide and my recovery was how naive I was at the time. I was still learning so much about how to utilize the tools from the 12-Step Program. I also had much to learn about what lay ahead in the Tour Divide and figured my participation in this race would likely allow me to learn more about myself. This certainly was the case, from the very first day.

Everything was perfect for Tour Divide, including the weather for the first few days. I was also happy that a cycling buddy had signed up to race, as it was nice to see a familiar face (Kent Murphy). And while we initially planned to

ride together we knew it is not only frowned upon per the rules of the Tour Divide (which require this to be a solo, self-supported effort), we also instinctively knew this was a recipe for disaster, as trying to have two people ride exactly alike, at the same pace, never really seems to work.

In fact, this is never a good plan. I share this perspective as it is also unrealistic when you consider that no two people want to stop at exact same time; ride at the exact same pace; eat at the exact same time, etc. You also need to factor in one's mood or how each is feeling each day, which is why Kent and I ultimately ended up riding at our own pace, but close enough to chat when the occasion arose.

The 2019 Tour Divide Race began at 8:00 a.m. as it historically does on the second Friday of every June (June 14th of 2019) with a slow, neutral ride out of Banff to a trail which would eventually become our home, for the next few days, weeks or months -- depending on pace. It did not take long for me to be totally blown away at how beautiful the course is. I truly did ride the whole first day with a smile on my face (except admittedly when going uphill, which became increasingly more common as each day evolved), as I was so happy to not only FINALLY begin to start RIDING (and get rid of some of the anxiousness that had been building for months), but now was able to see for myself how drop-dead beautiful this adventure was to become.

I was in heaven: biking, with a lengthy period of time-off from work, participating in the adventure of a lifetime! And while most photos do not usually do justice to the beauty of the subject, the photo below captures how truly spectacular and majestic the surroundings were.

However, despite my joy of riding in such beautiful surroundings, it was not long before I got lost. Yikes, as this was only the first hour of the race! This was stupid mistake number-one, as I was just not paying attention and missed a turn. I also was not very familiar with my *Garmin Etrex-30* (my navigation device that was pre-loaded with the entire course). Nor had I developed the important habit of occasionally looking down at my course instructions. No big deal though, as a ranger turned me around after about a mile down the wrong road, and got me back on course. Not a great way to start! Though, I was back on course and got back into a comfortable rhythm as I pedaled toward my first stop, about 50-miles into the day.

It was about this time that I made another major mistake, as I did not really load up with food for the afternoon, instead stocking up on just Gatorade. This became a huge mistake for me, as the sugar content really messes with my stomach on long journeys. Combined with the altitude, I began to feel sick to my stomach. In fact, I started to think about what a huge overall mistake this was to even be doing this race. I kept thinking "how in the hell was I going to be able to keep this up, especially if I felt awful like this every single day?"

To make matters worse, I never really hydrated with water along the way on the first day either (after my Gatorade was gone) as I should have. This was probably the most important lesson learned, as I never fully grasped the importance of stopping to obtain water along the way from the many mountain streams we encountered, as I figured we would run into more gas stations than actually existed (Note: I filtered all my water, being concerned about getting sick from stream germs as well). This mistake really came to fruition once I arrived at *Koko Claims*, an infamous mountain pass I dreaded the most, on day-one no less (though, I was pleased to complete 104-miles by 5:45 p.m. despite the late start on race day).

In my mind, "Koko" was the most ridiculous aspect of the whole race, though keep in mind I did not finish, so I am sure there are many other more ridiculous course sections out there. And, in fairness to those who routed the race up this long, steep, ridiculous rocky mountain pass -- this was done due to a bridge being washed away in the previous year -- or so I was told.

However, the mountain pass known simply as "Koko" is comprised of soccer-ball sized rocks; is extremely steep in sections; and goes on forever! When you are tired and dehydrated, the task of getting to the top is even more difficult.

In my case, this specific climb took over 4-hours to get to the top, all the while trying to push my 50-pound bike up the mountain, which got worse by the minute. In fact, at one point, I had to lay on the side of the trail, just to recover from the effort, as I had run out of water. Fortunately, riders were sharing some of their water with me. Though, as they passed, I could not have been more embarrassed from my unpreparedness, as I am sure they were all saying privately "this guy will never make it." Ironically, given my eventual outcome, they kind of had a point! Fortunately, my demise was short-lived as one woman came by and felt sorry for me, and shared a whole bottle of water, which truly saved the day.

This huge mistake was never repeated, as I learned the hard way how important it is to get water when you can, from mountain streams, as opposed to when it is too late! For me, I had started the climb up "Koko" knowing the need for water, but decided to pass up streams, thinking there would be another water source further up the mountain, when no other stream or water source  existed. Again, a huge mistake I was to never repeat. For me, I guess I like to learn the hard way!

As planned, I made it to the top of the mountain, where there was a nice, newer cycling cabin utilized by at least 10-15 other tired cyclists, for a good night's sleep. I was so glad day-one was over, with approximately 110-miles under my belt. I vowed the next day would be different. I was also super happy to not have to wake on day-two having to tackle the "Koko" climb, which was pretty much my motivation for going up this section on day one, so as to get this nasty section out of the way, in addition to the fact that there was a free cyclist cabin at the top.

The next morning, I awoke at sunrise, which to my surprise occurs at this time of the year at 5:00 a.m. (the sun sets late too, at around 10:00 p.m. which gives any rider at least 17-hours of sunlight to ride). The first order of business was to find a stream, to filter water to fill my bottles, to avoid a repeat of day-one, as I learned my lesson. However, repeated mistakes ensued, as I immediately missed a turn, again! It seems many people did, but within time, I was back on course soon and riding easily with others into the town of Fernie (Canada).

After a huge McDonalds breakfast, and some shopping for sandwich items (not knowing the next food stop), I was on my way. The miles churned by easily. At the end of day-two, I had ridden another 130-miles before retiring to camp for a second night. However, this is not to suggest the day was not without further drama, as this was the day I will always refer to as "The Great Bear Encounter" of 2019!

One of my greatest "fears" was encountering a bear. I knew the first week of the Tour Divide would place us in bear country and had hoped that the many stories I had heard about bear encounters did not materialize for me. Unfortunately, this was not to be the case, despite being fully prepared for an encounter with my bear spray. And, as most of the stories go, this occurs unexpectedly. In this situation, this was the case, as I was riding along with Kent on a wide fire-road (which incidentally was littered with bear poop, which should have been our first clue), when I was looking down and heard a scream from Kent. As I instantly looked up, I saw why Kent screamed. He was doing what everyone told us to do -- to scream, when you see a bear -- as we were told they are afraid of human voices.

The brown bear, which was approximately 50-yards ahead of us trying to cross the road, immediately turned around and darted back into the woods. That was it. *That was the great Bear Encounter of 2019.* However, I did learn what others also said: that bears are fast. In fact, this bear moved so quickly, that I wondered what the outcome would have been had the bear darted FOR US. Luckily, the scream scared the bear, and we were on our way. I would be less than honest to tell you that I was not looking around for bears more intently from this point forward, as I certainly was!

The second day ended having ridden 130-miles, with only approximately 30-miles to go to cross the United States/Canada border in the morning, which was the plan. Only one thing stood in our way: "The Wall." This was an extremely steep section of the route we were told was very challenging, necessitating lifting your heavy fully loaded bike up a muddy, steep incline.

Because we were extremely tired, it made sense to rest and tackle "The Wall" when we had more energy in the morning. And, because we were in the middle of nowhere, we had no choice other than to camp in the nature reserve where we found ourselves (near Wigwam, Canada), despite the fact that many bears existed in the area, which was obvious to us due to all the bear poop found along the path. Gulp!

After an uneventful but unnerving night sleeping in bear territory, we rose early to tackle "The Wall" and subsequently ride into the United States. In my mind, this was indeed a formidable challenge, but nothing compared to or as difficult as it was made out to be, especially when compared to the hike/bike of "Koko" which had been horrendous.

This also provided some comic relief, which Kent captured on some video of me grunting as I did my best to crawl up through the mud, with my bike in tow, to make it up the steep incline to conquer "The Wall." Once over the crest of this hill, we pedaled away knowing that another steep mountain, Galton Pass, awaited us -- with a descent into the United States, as we were so close to crossing the U.S.A. border. Within an hour, we crested Galton Pass, and descended into the United States of America!

CHAPTER TWO
2019 Tour Divide Race
Montana: Gorgeous Mountains & Steep Climbs

Roosville (US Border) to Lakeview (Red Rock Pass)
Approximately 710-miles (53,667 feet of elevation gain)

Once we descended down Galton Pass, now having conquered "The Wall" we then crossed into the United States to proceed through U.S. Customs. This was a special moment, which was captured by a courteous customs officer who enjoyed hearing about our adventure and snapped our photo.

This was an important milestone, as 267-miles were now under our belt well before noon, and most importantly, I was back in the United States! After a brief late Sunday morning brunch in the town of Eureka, the miles easily churned on. Ultimately, my third day of riding ended with another big day of 130+ miles, ending in the town of Whitefish, with a full 370-miles completed in just three days. Both Kent and I were pleased with our progress.

As I finished the third day of riding, I also remember being pleased with the fact that we had also gained (climbed) at least 28,275 feet in elevation, in addition to the mileage. This is the equivalent height of Mt. Everest. All in all, things were going well. It was also comforting to stay in a hotel in the beautiful town of Whitefish, which not only had a jacuzzi to soothe my aching muscles, but allowed for a good night's rest, along with the opportunity to devour an huge extra-large pizza. This is exactly what I needed, despite the fact that I started to notice a slight cough, which I summarily dismissed. In retrospect, little did I realize this was the beginning of the end for me, and it was only day three!

My fourth day began as many previous days did, with an early rise and on the road riding by 5:30 a.m. Again, the miles churned by easily, as I remember how happy I was to have an easy morning of paved roads, with little climbing. Like most days, this did not last for long as we soon were dumped on gravel roads, but the miles clicked by as I was totally enjoying the beauty of everything. This is where things took a turn for the worse weather-wise, as it began to get colder with occasional but short periods of rain.

I also began to feel the effects of illness, as my cough became more frequent, now combined with a sore throat. Again, this was the Tour Divide and knew there would be suffering, so I continued to climb through one mountain pass to the other, churning out the miles. And, when the occasion presented itself, I took advantage of the opportunity to eat a warm meal and have fun along the way.

In fact, I found time to goof around as Gumby, as this photo illustrates (subsequently posted on bikepacking.com). For me, this was essential -- to have fun along the way.

Aside from taking fun photos, I also enjoyed stopping for sit-down meals, not only because it was a great way to consume much needed calories, but also to meet other riders and to share "war stories" about our adventures. And, as all fun usually comes to an end, it was not long before I would hop right back on my bike to pedal on, and on, and on. This is a pattern that would be repeated daily, riding and climbing comfortably, but climbing at a rate of over 10,000+ feet per day, while also logging over 100+ miles per day. For me, an incredible accomplishment! Eventually, the day ended with another hotel in the vicinity of the town of Seeley Lake, after a late-night burger at a local pub, having now completed 503-miles (with over 40,525 feet of elevation gain) in just four days.

On day-five, I began to feel the effects of my daily high-mileage efforts, as my butt began to get sore. Go figure! I kept trying to convince myself this was not a big deal and part of the adventure, as I continued to apply cream onto my saddle areas. This helped -- but let me be candid: sitting on a saddle for 14-17 hours a day takes a toll. Part of the challenge, though, I figured! Again, the miles churned by easily.

By early afternoon, after making it over Huckleberry Pass and into the town of Lincoln for lunch (now having completed 567-miles by 2:00 p.m. on day-five), Kent and I pedaled away from town. Unfortunately, within a few miles, we ended up separating for reasons that had more to do with differing perspectives than anything else, which had intensified and become strained at times during the long days of riding together during challenging conditions.

Kent also had a knee injury that was really starting to bother him, whereas I felt fine. This led to a decision resulting in Kent camping on his own later that night, while I decided to forge ahead through the dark all alone, finishing at midnight in the state capital of Helena (about 20-miles further than Kent).

Once I separated from Kent and rode into the night, several realities set in. I came to realize I really did not like night riding, nor riding alone. To me, there was enough daylight to crank out some serious mileage during the day, without having to ride into the night. I also felt as if I had lost perspective and context for where I was, and navigation became much more difficult. I especially did not like navigating in the dark because it was hard enough to keep track of my directions in the light of day, let alone in the dark. And it was scary, being alone.

I also feared a situation at night similar to what happened to me earlier in the day, which really scared me. Earlier that day, I had been riding on my own and glanced down at my Garmin to make certain I was on the correct path, only to notice the Garmin was GONE! It must have popped off the handlebars. Yikes! Without navigation, I would be lost, with no real hope to find my way in very remote territory. So, I had no choice but to turn around and re-trace my steps.

Within 3-miles of turning around and looking for my navigation-device on the road, it was found. Whew! Disaster averted. I could not have even imagined how bad things could have been had this happened during the dark of night. Fortunately, this worked out, but when you are tired, this is not a funny matter.

As day came to an end, I decided to find another hotel, as I was in no mood to camp, and realized I had a love for the comforts of a hotel versus camping and stumbled upon a nice Motel 6 in the town of Helena. After a hot bath to soothe the muscles, I was fast asleep in a warm bed, which was a nice respite from the high mileage and significant climbing achieved, having now ridden 629-miles through five days of riding (and climbing 53,965 feet!). Again, all seemed well, yet my cough persisted and seemed to be getting worse. Not a big problem I told myself, as it was all part of the "deal" to compete in one of the longest, hardest mountain bike races in the world.

Despite ending the day feeling pretty good about having completed approximately 630-miles of my journey in just five days of riding, this is where I began to honestly become concerned. My cough and sore throat did indeed begin to have an impact -- subsequently changing my mindset. I wisely started to back-off on the higher mileage days, as I had noticed I was beginning to want to "call it quits" in the early evening hours (around 6:00 p.m.), as opposed to riding to sundown (10:00 p.m.). These were always very difficult decisions to make. But, the circumstances and availability of lodging, as opposed to being in a cold tent if I was to ride past a town with a hotel, dictated my decision-making process for when to call it a day, along with the fact I thought it was wise, in the interest of allowing myself more time to physically recover.

The next and sixth day of riding began as I went up Grizzly Gulch and Lava Mountain alone, as Kent was no longer with me. As I climbed up Lava Mountain, I remember sarcastically wondering why it was called this. After experiencing the un-rideable hike/bike section littered with lava-like rocks, I had my answer. I rode when I could and walked when it made sense, to the top. Once at the top, as was always the case throughout this whole ordeal, I enjoyed yet another descent which had become common, and my favorite part of the journey, especially since I didn't have to pedal for what seemed like endless periods of time. It was after Lava Mountain that I went into the town of Basin, and had another sit-down warm meal.

It was at this point that Kent appeared in the distance, as he was behind me all morning. This reunion was sooner than I would have thought since separating the previous day. Fortunately, I was able to draw upon some of the lessons learned during my years in sobriety as I stopped my bike and approached Kent to apologize. We both felt uncomfortable about our disagreements the previous day and were able to find the right words to apologize and make amends. Thank God too for answered prayers, as I missed riding with Kent, and did not like riding alone. All of the tools I learned in sobriety (prayer, making amends, forgiveness, and admitting one's mistakes) are not only helpful in situations like this, but are used daily as I continue to remain sober, one day at a time.

After we came to terms with our differences, together we hit the next six smaller mountain passes that lay ahead (not as daunting as it sounds, as they were not as long as previous climbs), into the town of Butte. Given how I was feeling, it seemed to make sense to make this an easier day, to help recover from my sore throat. Thus, the day was a short rest day of just 80-miles, as we rode into Butte to find another hotel after visiting the local bike shop for an inspection of my bike. This also gave me a chance to do some laundry and stock up on food for another early morning departure the next day. I remember being somewhat bummed that I had cut the day short at 6:00 p.m., but practically speaking was quite pleased that I still had covered approximately 710 miles over six days of riding, and having climbed over 61,000+ feet. This still put me a full-day ahead of a 22-day finish pace, which was my goal, so no harm.

I left Butte well rested, due to the short easy day prior, which really helped. I was also very pleased with my progress, though I vowed I would not allow myself to have another day of anything less than 100+ miles. This was not to be the case though, as I woke up still coughing, but now with a really sore throat. Again, not a big deal, as it was an expectation that suffering is part of the equation when you participate in ultra-distance races like this. So, I forged on. What made things more cheerful was running into other riders along the way, which allowed me to develop some nice friendships with other familiar cyclists on the route, depending on where they slept or where they stopped to eat.

At this point in the race, this is where conditions became "real fun" (sarcasm intended) as the weather was no longer nice, but began to get cold, windy and much more challenging, with occasional rain. However, I was always super prepared, having clothes for every condition. The problem though is that I was constantly stopping to change clothes, depending on conditions. Smart-riding I thought, but frustrating to Kent, who occasionally would forge ahead only for me to constantly have to catch up. Again, I learned it is probably best to just do my own thing. It probably also did not help that I felt like I was getting Kent sick, or perhaps he was getting me sick, as we both had a rough cough, now getting worse by the day. As we rode on, and did some further climbing, snow flurries began to appear. With each pedal stroke up the mountains, flurries came in what best can be described a "mini blizzard" atop the mountain! I changed clothing to descend, but nonetheless froze (especially my hands) by the time I got to the bottom.

By now, a few of us were riding together, as we forged into the next town for a group lunch with about six other riders. The camaraderie from the Tour Divide is what I loved most (and misery does indeed love company). After a much-needed meal, I pedaled into yet another long slog up another steep mountain, but this time for an unforgettable "white-out" at the top, leaving me totally covered in snow by the descent. This descent was not fun, as my hands were frozen, and by the bottom of the mountain I was definitely counting the miles until I could shelter in the warm confines of the High Country Lodge, which was the ideal stop for the day, and my favorite spot on the trip.

The hospitality at the High Country Lodge was second to none: great people, great food, warm beds, other riders, and food for the next day's journey, which was another long stretch of at least 100-miles before we would be able to replenish food.

We woke to a hearty, warm breakfast at the High Country Lodge. It was a true blessing for the energy needed for that day's journey, forecast with flurries and rain. This would not be an easy day, despite the fact that we had very little climbing to do, but still had at least 100-miles to cover until we could replenish food in the town of Lima. However, despite my spirits being positive, my sore throat was now becoming *a major concern*. I was praying that by mid-day, I would feel better, which was becoming a familiar pattern of wishful thinking. Despite all these challenges, l still did my very best to have fun along the way, as this photo illustrates, stumbling upon a ranch with my last name!

However, my sore throat was no longer my only concern. As I continued to gain some serious elevation, the altitude was really beginning to affect me (I am a 56-year-old sea-level guy from Cleveland, OH). And while the journey to get to Lima was seemingly flat, with some rolling hills, it did not include the types of tough climbs earlier experienced. This was a great relief. But, for some reason I started to feel like I was "out of it" and riding in "slow-motion." The elevation played a big part of this condition, despite my belief that I had been acclimating to the elevation well. And the wear and tear also was beginning to take a serious toll on my body.

As usual, I rested if a breather was needed, but was beginning to really notice a definite change in health. This became very apparent during long descents, as was the case going through some amazing caverns on my way to Lima, because I was still feeling short of breath. Though, I trudged on and got to Lima by late afternoon, without any real plan for the remainder of the day, as it was now about 5:00 p.m.

Eventually, after a late afternoon burger, we saw a storm ahead in the mountains, right in the path of where we were headed. While Kent and I both wanted to forge ahead, after consulting with a local sheriff familiar with the expected weather, a decision was made to call it a day with another 100-miles under our belts. Nor did it make sense to ride into the rain, only to have to set-up and break-down camp in the rain, as sick as we both felt. This was not an easy decision for either of us, as we debated this point endlessly. Ultimately, as other riders were making the decision to call it quits for the day too, five of us decided to get a cabin and share a room. Unfortunately for our roommates, they heard both Kent and me coughing all night, which was a precursor for what was to come the next day.

The next day, after an awful night's coughing, I woke up to not only a sore throat, but now *I could not swallow*. This was as bad as it had been all trip. I had thought about calling it quits, as I saw a nearby highway which I was certain could take me to a larger city and a doctor. That was the prudent thing to do. But, like any crazy Tour Divide rider on-the-clock, it was unimaginable for me to waste precious time. So, I foolishly awakened and just began to pedal, with the hope I would "just get better." This was not to be the case.

Now, the miles felt slow. Real slow. I also *could not drink fluids due to the fact I could not swallow*, which I knew was the kiss of death. Then, I came upon a section of road that was nothing but pure mud, with the consistency of peanut butter, which caked my tires to the point they could not even move. Resorting to lifting my bike while trudging through the mud, I now started to consider dropping out. Somehow, I got through the mud and just started to pedal. Unfortunately, the seed of quitting had now been planted in my head, and it did not go away. I did my best, but it was tough to swallow, making it hard to hydrate. Combined with saddle sores, hip soreness, cold weather, and other issues related to the wear and tear from my nine-day 1,000-mile journey...it was time to call it quits.

I really cannot remember the exact moment, but as I was walking my bike for a quick break, I noticed a pick-up truck on the horizon. When the truck neared, and without even really thinking it through, I instinctively waved him down. *It happened that quick. My Tour Divide was officially over.* I asked the driver if I could hitch a ride to the next town, and he kindly obliged. I turned off my satellite tracker, threw my bike in his pick-up and was on my way home. But, it would not be that easy. As we drove down the road, I remember how bad I felt physically, but even worse compared to the regret I felt from allowing myself to quit so easily.

Despite regret, my decision was made. As we drove down the road with my bike in the back of the pick-up truck, I then saw Kent pedaling away, and we stopped so I could tell him of my decision. Incidentally, Kent finished his ride that day, but after a full day's rest, he rode for one more day and then called it quits too, due to his illness as well. After a quick goodbye, we drove on. Ultimately, my savior in the pick-up truck was headed in another direction, and he dropped me off so I could pedal six-miles to a town. Good enough for me, as I had a plan to get to a hotel and rest, and then get to a large city the next day with an airport, so I could fly home.

After the short ride and in no mood to get lost, another pick-up truck drove by, so I decided to ask for confirmation of my directions. The two men in the truck, who had been fishing that day in the area, asked what I was doing and where I was eventually headed. I told them I needed to get to a city with an airport. Lucky for me, they told me they were headed to Idaho Falls, and that I could throw my bike in the truck and take me there. This was a blessing in disguise, and I took them up on their offer. Within two hours, I was in a hotel room in Idaho Falls, booking my flight home. *Just like that, my Tour Divide was OVER!*

Once settled into my room at the hotel, I took the time to share the following news on *facebook* of my decision to drop out, on Day 9 (after 977-miles and 77,707 feet of climbing):

I am disappointed to report that I had to drop-out of The Tour Divide due to worsening health. I got sick a few days into the race and it got worse daily – to the point where it was tough to swallow (making it hard to drink/hydrate). Combined with saddle sores, hip soreness; cold weather and other issues related to the wear and tear from my nine-day 1,000-mile journey…it was time to call it quits. Disappointed, but I just decided it made sense long-term to drop-out. The GOOD NEWS is that I was able to raise over $3,220 for the Cystic Fibrosis Foundation (a cause near & dear to my heart) thru my participation in the Cycle-For-Life Program, thanks to the generosity of so many. Thank you all for your support!!!

Despite the tough decision to drop out, I never allowed myself to feel totally defeated by the Tour Divide and am still quite proud of my effort. I am proud that I trained and rode well. I also was part of an incredible experience that allowed me to see some amazing sights along the route, in a gorgeous part of the country, which I would have never seen in my lifetime, had I not participated. I also gained a spiritual connection like I had never experienced before in my life, which was comforting, and helpful in my recovery.

What also made my journey worthwhile was the fact that I was also able to help raise funds for the Cystic Fibrosis Foundation. In fact, both Kent and I raised over $4,000 toward the cause. *That alone is reason to celebrate!* This achievement also reflects one of the most important actionable principles of my recovery program, which is to help others.

However, I would be less than honest if I tried to convince you I was pleased with the decision to drop out. I was not happy with this outcome, nor am I to this day, as I did not finish, and know I was capable and in shape to complete my journey. I share this despite the realization that I join a long list of others who attempted as rookies and did not finish. Even some big names in the sport, and many others of the "2019 race leaders" dropped out as well, either due to weather, or other factors. Though, along with the other 60+ percent of people who started and did not finish (common for this race), my situation and experience was as different from theirs.

As I reflect on this experience, I still feel some regret for what still in my mind was the ultimate DNF (Did Not Finish), that I had quit way too easily. I also feared quitting might become an easy habit that might become an instinctive learned response when things got tough in my recovery. That frightened me.

Though, given my physical condition, which was subsequently confirmed by my physician when I returned home, I realized I was being too tough on myself, as I had an illness that required antibiotics, which ultimately returned me to full health within a week. Gosh, I wondered -- what if I took antibiotics on the trip, could I have perhaps gotten better...and finished? It was not meant to be. And, there is always next year!

In my mind, the seed was still planted, but had not yet a chance to fully blossom. Clearly, my adventure was not over. In that respect, it was only a matter of time before I would return to complete my ride, hopefully with a stronger mindset from an additional year in recovery. Finishing this ride would also serve as reaffirmation of the necessary mindset needed to remain sober, and to never quit, as I have now learned and practice every day, one day at a time.

As it turned out, that day came almost a full year later, when I returned in mid-May of 2020, as the constant thought of completing MY ADVENTURE consumed me. I had to finish this ride, on the Great Divide!

CHAPTER THREE

2020 Great Divide Ride

Frustration "On The Road To Glory"

"Dreams are today's answers to tomorrow's questions."

Edgar Cayce

It was now May 15, 2020. After a full year of guilt from dropping out of the 2019 Tour Divide, I had enough. I needed to finish this ride, regardless of a worldwide pandemic!

My desire to complete the Great Divide, as explained earlier, was now in full swing. My journey began at Cleveland Hopkins Airport. *This was one of the many days I dreaded, as I had to travel with my bike on an airplane, which is never an easy thing.* My anxiety level was also at an all-time high, as my fear of Covid-19 was magnified by the restrictions placed upon each passenger. Everyone had to wear masks, which might seem to alleviate my fears, but candidly, it served as nothing more than a constant reminder that the virus was everywhere. However, I did everything to mitigate risk of infection, following every infection prevention protocol.

To make matters worse, I knew that when I was to arrive in Denver at 3:00 p.m., my ultimate journey would become complicated, as I had to rent a car to begin my ten-hour drive from Denver to Yellowstone National Park, the starting point in Wyoming where I planned to begin biking the next day. I had also planned to begin in the early morning, as I had an 80-mile ride to complete on the first day of my adventure. Wishful thinking, as it turned out.

Fortunately, the flight was uneventful. I felt safe, although I must have used a whole bottle of hand-sanitizer wiping down every single surface in and near my seat on the plane. The transition from the plane to car rental location went seemingly well, despite having to haul my bike in a box through the airport to the bus, and then to the car rental counter. After the usual hassle of paperwork to get the car, I needed to open the bike box and begin to assemble key components of the bike to load into the car. For those who travel with their bike on a plane, this is a pain in the butt, and creates stress.

Additionally, aside from a ten-hour car ride to my ultimate destination, the looming thought of the ride the next day added further anxiety. I was stressed. In fact, when I spoke to my wife and some other friends about my progress, they too commented how I sounded stressed out. The car ride did not help. I just wanted to pedal my bike.

Despite all the anxiety, with the bike partially assembled and in the rental car, I drove away from the Denver Airport and started to feel good about the fact that my airplane travel was now completed. It was now time to tackle my ten-hour car ride to Yellowstone, which was near the Montana/Wyoming border. As I traveled along the major interstate that intersected the Great Divide trail, I noticed the barren land that was to become my home for the next four to six days, after starting to ride. I also noticed the incredibly strong winds, and signs warning about "strong winds." At the time, little did I realize this would become a challenge of the ride that would come to haunt me.

As I continued to drive and make good time heading northwest to Yellowstone, I noticed a sporting goods store and decided to stop to buy bear-spray. This was an essential stop, as I knew the first several days of the cycling journey would be in bear territory and needed to be prepared. Bear spray was an essential recommended survival item I could not ride without, as wild animals along the 1,700-mile journey were routine. This was a concern. In fact, my initial first planned day of riding would take me through Yellowstone, which had been closed for months due to the pandemic. During this time, I had seen many online videos showing the animals (bears, bison, etc.) running wild within the park, given that people had not been visiting. In that respect, I viewed my initial ride through Yellowstone as more dangerous than usual. Nonetheless, I really wanted to ride through this national treasure, and visit the iconic "Old Faithful" geyser, despite the perceived danger.

Another element of stress was the uncertainty of *exactly* where to start my ride. This would not be fully determined until I got into the area due to a whole host of factors, including the changing impact of the Covid-19 pandemic, which would have ramifications throughout my adventure. Just my unfortunate luck, Yellowstone National Park was closed, as I arrived in the area a mere two days before it was to officially open. And while I was initially under the impression I could ride through the park on a state road that ran through the park, conflicting information provided by local residents suggested otherwise, as the gated entrance to my planned route was closed.

To make matters worse, I was also informed by local residents that my secondary plan of riding south of Yellowstone, through Idaho and over a vital mountain pass to the town of Jackson Hole, Wyoming, was impassable, due to mud and snow. Thus, both my starting point as planned and my "Plan B" were not working.

Another complication in the decision of where to start my ride involved return of my rental car. Once my plans changed, there were few alternative rental car drop-off options. After several hours of frustrating phone calls to arrange an alternate rental car drop-off, which would add to my already tiring ten-hour drive, I made the decision to abandon my initial plan and return to Jackson Hole. This is an area I had previously driven through two-hours earlier, where an alternative rental car drop-off location existed. By the time I arrived back in Jackson Hole, it was now 1:00 p.m. I had now turned an expected four-hour morning drive into an unexpected eight-hour debacle. Not a good way to start the first day of riding.

Once I returned the car in Jackson Hole, it was time to ride, or so I thought. I now had to *fully assemble* my bike with all my gear for the 80-mile ride to my first day destination: Pinedale, Wyoming. Unfortunately, to add to the growing list of frustrations, the revised plan now involved an immediate route deviation. Because I was riding much earlier in the year than the start of the Tour Divide, which occurs in mid-June when most of the mountain passes are clear, I had to be constantly mindful that certain sections of the Great Divide trail still might have mud and snow in the mountains.

Indeed, local residents in Jackson Hole confirmed that Union Pass, the first expected section of the ride, was impassable. For that reason, I needed to ride the road around this section of the Great Divide in order to reach Pinedale. Ultimately, the route deviation I chose was beautiful, as I traveled along the Hoback River, through the Bridger-Teton National Forest.

Finally, before even beginning my adventure, I also had to contend with a mechanical issue that occurred within the first 100-yards of riding. Yes, the first 100-yards of my journey! As I began to pedal, I noticed the front brake was squeaking noticeably which also affected how the wheel rolled. This did not surprise me, as I had a hard time getting the wheel installed at the airport car rental counter, and noticed something awry, likely from my impatience and being desperate to start pedaling. I thought to myself "Could this get any worse," as I already needed a bike shop for a repair!

Fortunately, there was a bike shop right around the corner. And the good news: once I pulled up, they seemed to discern the obvious anguish on my face, being fully loaded for a long journey, and waved me to the front of a lengthy line, to immediately assess and fix the problem. It turned out to be a spring near the brake pad that needed to be replaced. I also caught another fortunate "break" (excuse the obvious pun…), as I had brought a spare part and tool necessary for a quick fix. I was grateful for good preparedness, with spare parts and the right tool for every scenario.

This became a common lesson throughout the ride that closely parallels every aspect of my recovery, which is to access *tools* available for each unique situation in life. Moreover, the *tools* I have learned during my sobriety, over the course of the past four years since entering the AA Program, have become essential elements for common problems that occur not only during cycling endeavors, but each day of my life, which I approach one day at a time.

My frustrations experienced along the way also reminded me of another important lesson I constantly work to address, which is to utilize the *tools* learned from the 12-Step Program.

An important lesson indeed, as MY ADVENTURE had now begun. I was now finally on my bike, ready to live my adventure.

RECOVERY

DOESN'T MEAN MY PROBLEMS GO AWAY....

...IT JUST MEANS I HAVE THE TOOLS TO DEAL WITH THEM!

CHAPTER FOUR

2020 Great Divide Ride

Wyoming: My "Windy" Journey Begins

Jackson Hole to Baggs - Wyoming
Approximately 415-miles (24,451 feet of elevation gain)

Finally, as I began to pedal away from Jackson Hole, my anxiety began to ease with each stroke of the pedal. It was as if the weight of the world had now lifted, and I could do what I came to do -- just ride my bike. For me, I realize sheer joy when I am cycling, as a sense of freedom and purpose begins to enter my psyche. However, despite the apparent smile on my face, within a few miles, my glee turned to reality as I began to calculate what lay ahead. This was the moment when I not only began to question why I was doing this in the first place, but also the first opportunity in which the "demons of doubt in my head" began to resurface as the whole 1,700-mile journey started to come into focus.

This is where the approach to each day's ride became a challenge, as it is easy to overwhelm oneself with the larger challenge that always lies ahead. In that respect, a common occurrence for me is that when I begin to focus on thinking of the larger picture, it is easy to find excuses for not being able to accomplish the task at hand, and I begin to find convenient excuses to quit. And I did want to quit, which is ironic because I had only just begun.

This is the same challenge I have found in my recovery program, as it is easy to become overwhelmed with the thought that I must never drink again, for the rest of my life! But, when you break down that daunting challenge in terms of what can be accomplished, on any given day, as opposed to focusing on the bigger picture, any challenge becomes more manageable.

That is where the tools brought forth from the AA 12-Step Program (see Appendix 4) come into play, to just take it *one day at a time*. This is also the attitude I employ in cycling, which was utilized on my first day in order to complete my 80-mile ride to get to Pinedale, as it is all about just pedaling, or moving forward, one day at a time.

> ## *LIFE IS LIKE RIDING A BICYCLE; TO KEEP YOUR BALANCE, YOU MUST KEEP MOVING FORWARD.*

This approach not only got me through my first day, but every day thereafter, despite the negativity about the whole 1,700-mile journey that began to creep into my head. Within time, despite the distance and climbing necessary to get to my destination, combined with the fact that I also got a late start which was less than ideal, I made it to my day-one destination.

I also was able to find peace in the beauty of my ride along the Hoback River through the Bridger-Teton National Park, which was effortless. This peace also served as a reminder of a "fulfilled promise" that I would consistently experience during the ride, consistent with the 12-Promises of AA (see Appendix 5) that persons in recovery experience while working the 12-

Step Program. In fact, on many occasions throughout my Great Divide ride, I was able to reflect and begin to appreciate, through the lens of recovery, some "promise type" outcomes experienced during the ride that resulted from working the 12-Steps, during my four-years of recovery (such as spiritual contentment, peacefulness, usefulness, positive thinking, and unselfishness).

With this inner-peace, I truly began to enjoy the view of the snow-covered mountains, while also being able to observe the joy of others kayaking and rafting down the river as I traveled through the Bridger-Teton National Forest. All in all,  my first day ended on a positive note, as I arrived in Pinedale around 8:00 p.m., found a hotel, and went to sleep, ready for the second day of riding.

Upon awakening the next day, for the first full day without having to deal with the hassle of airplane or car travel, I could now instead just ride my bike. Everything was perfect, until I went for a coffee and…locked the hotel key in my room! Ugh. However, after a phone call to the local owner of the hotel, who quickly came to the rescue, I was on my way from Pinedale to Atlantic City, on the Great Divide trail.

Again, the ride was effortless, as I headed out of town on a smooth road before entering onto a gravel section approximately 15-miles into the 85-mile expected ride for the day. It was at this point that I truly began to appreciate the remote yet beautiful aspects of this trail: snow covered mountains, wildlife, gorgeous plains, and numerous hills which accentuated the landscape.

I also began to take in my surroundings and take photos, which illustrated that I was keeping the proper perspective on the ride. Even though I exhibited a tendency to ride faster than necessary, I told myself to chill and "take in" the scenery and did so at every opportunity.

And while the scenery was indeed beautiful, the heat also became a problem. Fortunately, there was ample water along the way, which minimized my agony, as the miles clicked by. When I needed water, I would just stop at the occasional creek or stream and cleanse the water with my water filter, so that it was free of any contamination or germs.

Additionally, I stopped on occasion to say hello to non-cyclists who were also on the trail, most often tending to their cattle, or enjoying the weekend. Within a matter of hours, and after enjoying some tunes I had programmed on my I-tunes playlist, the miles really clicked by. It was just a matter of time before I was in South Pass City, an old historic gold mine city that was now closed due to the pandemic.

That didn't stop me, though, from becoming the ultimate tourist, as I explored all the town had to offer: an old general store; the Carissa Gold Mine; a town square complete with a mercantile store (Wyoming's first masonic lodge); and on my way out of  town, a boarded-up mine (which I could not resist to explore)!

Once I had fulfilled my adventuring spirit in South Pass City, I hopped back on my bike to my eventual destination: Atlantic City, and a night at Wild Bill's Gun Shop & Cabins. This stop certainly did not disappoint, as when I arrived in Atlantic City, which was just a few miles up the road, I met the man himself: Wild Bill.

My stay at Wild Bill's was one of the highlights of my second leg of this trip, as he was one of the most kind, informative and gregarious hosts one could ever hope to meet. He was gracious enough to set me up for the night in one of the many cabins on his property. Within a few hours of settling into my cabin, I sat with Bill for several hours learning everything I could from him about life in Wyoming: ranching, hunting, western politics, and every other topic over which our conversation seemed to wander. What really had the most impact on me, though, was Wild Bill's honesty, and his faith in God. This truly humbled and touched me. I also found myself opening up and sharing with Bill my struggles with alcohol, and how this trip was an opportunity for me to search my soul and find purpose and strengthen my recovery. What was truly remarkable about this candid exchange was the fact that we were total strangers to one another. This is what makes this trail, and the people you meet along the way, such an incredible experience. The generosity expressed to me, too, was incredible.

After a hearty dinner, it was off to bed in my cozy cabin, as I knew the next day's ride would be one of my toughest, with the ride through the Great Basin and its feared headwinds. Indeed, I had been reminded how tough the wind would be during my entire visit at Wild Bill's. All night long, the wind never seemed to stop blowing; and as I slept, the sound of the wind was deafening. Typical for this area.

However, despite the roar of wind, I had a good night's sleep, ready for the next day's adventure. At breakfast, Bill and I continued our conversation right where we left off the night before, but now with his wife, in their kitchen. She prepared an amazingly full plate of pancakes, sausage, eggs and toast. They made sure I was fully loaded with energy, and surely needed it, as day-three required a 100-mile ride through the Great Basin.

The Great Basin is not only a flat monotonous stretch of land between Atlantic City and my destination to Wamsutter, but also a vast open stretch with no shade and historically high winds. When cycling, this is the kiss of death. Additionally, there is limited water throughout this desolate stretch, and aside from some incredible sightings of wildlife, it is nothing more than gravel road and sagebrush. In some respects, it can be beautiful. However, without water, it was a dangerous portion of the Great Divide. For me, with a personal history of not physically performing well in the heat, my anxiety level was at an all-time high.

As I left Atlantic City, after a short steep climb, I knew I needed to find a well (water source) located exactly 20.6 miles into the journey. Unfortunately, after riding 22-23 miles, I must have missed the well. Not a good omen. Panic began to set in as I turned around to find the well. I checked my map, which I always kept in my pocket to identify key course markings, but to no avail. I must have spent 30-minutes back and forth looking for the well. Ultimately, I came to realize that if I did not find this well, I would not have enough water to make it through the Great Basin, and would have to return to Atlantic City, which would have really complicated my overall journey.

Fortunately, within an hour, I found the well. It was marked with an animal skull on the road, and some sticks on the ground in the shape of an arrow, seemingly innocuous markers for such a life-sustaining source! Bummed-out about losing an hour, I now reloaded with water and decided to forge ahead. This was only the beginning of this challenging day, as it was starting to get hot. Temperatures were in the 90's, and the winds were in my face, making cycling even harder. For a cyclist, headwinds are dreaded as much as rain and cold, and amplify the struggle.

I continued to pedal until I got to the middle of the Great Basin and looked around. I was all alone. I was also in the middle of nowhere and had not seen a soul for hours. This is when the fear of being alone really becomes increasingly scary. However, fear was not my only concern. After being on a gravel road which was sandy and a total washboard (bumpy), I was then diverted to a rocky trail that then lead to a trail that looked like it hadn't been traveled on since the stagecoaches last traveled in 1880. Was I lost? Additionally, the afternoon winds really began to pick up, and were now close to 30-mph, making riding so much more difficult.

It was at this point that I reflected upon my 12-Step Program. I realized that I had conquered challenges far more difficult than this. From that perspective, I knew I would be fine and make it to my daily destination. And this was indeed my first real challenging day, although there would be many more ahead.

I forged ahead, but that wind sure was tough. At one point, and on several occasions thereafter, I found respite by hiding from the wind and sun under an occasional oil-pipe that was scattered throughout the landscape.

I also found a real old but cool abandoned log cabin next to a pond. It also happened to have a huge eagle nest inside, that fortunately for me, did not contain an eagle ready to attack.

This cabin was a Godsend, as I loaded up with water; whenever I could, I would always take advantage of a water source and re-load. Eventually, after about nine to ten hours of riding, I made it out of the Great Basin with a *Love's Truck Stop* in Wamsutter appearing on the horizon.

Never have I been so happy to see a truck stop. Once I arrived, I sucked down a few cokes and chocolate milks, and made my way to a hotel to collapse, rest, and eat; in preparation for what I thought would be an easy and flat 100-mile ride the next day. Little did I realize, this was not to be the case, as the wind continued to pick up through the night and into the next day.

Upon awakening, I held off eating a big meal, determining it would not take me long to crank out the first 50-miles to Baggs. Making my way down yet another gravel road, I realized what a mistake it was to pass on my morning meal and essential fuel, as this section took forever. Once again, just like the Great Basin, the winds were ridiculously fierce. I had hoped to have an easy ride, but this was not meant to be. Endlessly, I pedaled, and pedaled, and pedaled -- constantly trying to brace against the wind, which never let up at 25-30 miles per hour -- right into my face.

It should be pointed out the route I chose on this day was yet another deviation off the Great Divide trail, because I needed to head into Steamboat Springs, Colorado for my arrival the next day. There, I had planned to meet my good friend Rob Andrew (who lives in Boulder), and who had committed to ride with me for three to four days while in Colorado.

The rationale for my route deviation was also based on "playing it safe" as I had been informed that the next section on the Great Divide trail from Wamsutter to Steamboat Springs had a closure at the Brush Mountain Lodge, due to the pandemic, and was also the section where the previous year's Tour Divide race had been halted due to treacherous mud and impassable snow. I knew I would face the same outcome.

Thus, I decided to ride from Wamsutter, Wyoming to Craig, Colorado on the road. Despite the additional challenge of having to navigate a gravel road route I had created, I felt some satisfaction knowing this day would allow me to realize an important and significant milestone, as I would be leaving Wyoming (and bid "good-riddens" to the fierce winds) and enter Colorado! A significant achievement, indeed. However, this was not easily earned, as yet again I had to stop on occasion to hide from the sun, and rest from the wind; which, after hours and hours of pounding me on the bike, clearly added to fatigue, and mental anguish.

Eventually, I made it to the town of Baggs, which is at the Wyoming and Colorado border, and had a huge lunch. There, I met an incredibly kind and conversational waitress, which yet again reminded me that the best part of my adventure was meeting great people. I now had another 50-miles to go to Craig, and within minutes of leaving the restaurant, I saw the state sign welcoming me to Colorado. I was so relieved to have one of three states out of the way.

At this point, upon entering Colorado, I really felt that I had accomplished a lot, as I had ridden close to 415-miles in four days, with a little over 24,000+ feet of climbing. Combined with the fact that I was leaving "Windy Wyoming" I was excited to be entering Colorado. Within minutes, the whole landscape changed.

As I headed toward Craig, seemingly out of nowhere I began to see green emerging from the trees. A refreshing site, although I still had 50-miles to go, and the 30 mile per hour headwind continued its destructive domination over me and my bike. Though, I was so glad to be in Colorado!

CHAPTER FIVE

2020 Great Divide Ride

Colorado: Mountains & Altitude

From the Wyoming Border to New Mexico Border
Approximately 525-miles (27,415 feet of elevation gain)

After mid-day lunch, I entered Colorado. For me, a photograph in front of each state's "Welcome Sign" was mandatory, as it signified a new set of adventures on my ride. In terms of

Colorado, this meant mountains and altitude. Until now, the mountains I had climbed had been merely rolling hills. Nor would anything thus far compare to the steep climbs of Montana I had experienced the year before in the Tour Divide, as those climbs were tough, long and hard. I had also heard that the climbs in Colorado were not as steep, but instead had a more manageable gradient, but still seemingly endless. This was a welcome change. However, the altitude of Colorado was one of my greatest fears, as I had a poor track-record in races above 9,000+ feet (I had previously participated in the Leadville 100-mile Mountain Bike Race [12,600 feet]; and the Gunnison Growler [9,000+ feet] and did poorly, due to the altitude and its effect on me).

Within time, and with some perseverance, I made it to the town of Craig. This was not an easy day, but once again I persevered as a result of newfound strength that originated from some of the lessons I have learned from my 12-Step Program, and in particular, the ability to pray for strength in situations in which I am powerless over unmanageable situations. In this circumstance, as much as I despised the wind, I came to realize I needed to embrace the challenge, as there was really nothing which I could do about it anyway. That is the way weather is. Some days it is great, other days it is not. Needless to say, once arriving in Craig, I was so relieved the day was over; and found a local hotel to rest, recover and eat for fueling the next day's ride, which would be a super-easy day.

At this point in my adventure, I had some fun days in store that I had planned and had been looking forward to. In fact, my friend Rob Andrew had coordinated some unique places for me to stay (off-route), but I needed to kill time until we could coordinate our schedules. This meant getting to Steamboat Springs to wait for his arrival the next evening. This also allowed me an opportunity to rest for a day and half, until he arrived. As mentioned, this also required riding from Craig to Steamboat Springs, an easy 42-mile ride. Fortunately, the wind was now at my back, and I seemingly "flew" to Steamboat in less than two-hours riding time. You will never hear me complain about the wind when it is at my back!

However, I did not lose sight of what this journey was all about, which was to have fun. In that respect, before leaving town, at the local chamber of commerce, I noticed an old pullman train car custom-built in 1906 named "The Marcia"; named for the daughter of David Moffit, who was a famous Denver financier and industrialist. Never one to pass up a free museum tour, I stopped to view this unique town treasure, replete with every luxury available during that time period.

For me, diversions like this were what distinguished this ride along the Great Divide, from the Tour Divide race the previous year. The latter was a race in which you could ill-afford to waste time sight-seeing. Additionally, stops like this were the first time I began to really appreciate my new approach to this type of non-competitive riding, as it gave me time to have fun and "smell the roses" along the way.

After the train-car tour I was on my way, arriving in Steamboat Springs less than two-hours later. It seemed like a different world, as the experience in this town was unlike any I had experienced thus far, due to the pandemic.

Steamboat Springs was a town hard-hit by Covid-19. As a ski-resort, visitors always brought an infusion of revenue and economic development to the town from the ski-season, but they also brought something else with them this past year: Covid-19. As a result, I had to be extra sensitive in this situation, and respectful of the wishes of the local citizenry. As was the case with all previous encounters on the ride, I brought and wore a mask wherever and whenever the situation dictated. The impact on me and my adventure was felt immediately, as the local hotels were not offering rooms, unless you were an "essential worker." This restriction was also enforced at the local campgrounds, as those were closed too. This was a serious challenge, as I needed housing.

However, as I rode through town, I noticed a local hotel owner in the lobby of his hotel waving at me, and gesturing to come into his lobby. He knew by my appearance (and gear on my bike, as hundreds of annual riders like me come through this town) that I might be looking for a room. Indeed, I was. After responding to his question as to whether I was "essential" (to which I immediately replied "Of course I am essential," with a smart-aleck tone), I signed some kind of document that resulted in keys to a room. Alas, I had a place to stay. Now, I could kill the rest of the afternoon and the entire next day, being in a "wait and rest mode" to coordinate my visit with Rob. He too had also arranged for a place to stay the next evening, so we could ride with another friend of his, John, from his ranch in Steamboat Springs.

This was my first full rest day, despite the easy 42-mile ride earlier in the day. And although I wanted to keep riding from a mental standpoint, the rest would allow me to recover. I also wanted a chance to check out Steamboat Springs, as it was one of the iconic ski-towns along the Great Divide worthy of exploration, to see what the town had to offer. This is exactly what I did, as I toured local hot-spots, visited bike-shops, watched kayakers negotiate the river, and "bopped-around" town on my bike, just sight-seeing. I also had arranged with the hotel owner for a late departure, as my rendezvous with Rob was not to occur until he arrived in town via a rental car after 6:00 p.m. At that point, I had planned to ride an easy 15-miles on the Great Divide trail to his friend's ranch.

Hopping back on my bike the next day, I was fully rested and ready to ride again, recovered after a day's rest, to head to John's ranch. This sure was worth the wait.

The next evening, upon arriving at "Lazy C's Ranch," I was blown away by the beauty of this 300+ acre paradise. I was also overjoyed to see my good friend, Rob Andrew. Rob was one of my friends from college who participated on all my crazy college endeavors that landed us in the Guinness Book of World Records (in particular, our 53-day trampoline marathon; and 600-mile bathtub push - see Appendix 1). Both John and Rob, established cyclists, had planned to join my journey the next day. Rob would then continue riding with me for three to four days, until we landed in the area near Crested Butte, where he and his wife Siga, whom I also knew from college, had a second home. This was a plan that differed significantly from riding in the Tour Divide the previous year, as that was a race, and during a race you had little time to waste. Given the current circumstances with the race being cancelled and Covid-19 affecting food re-supply stops along the way, this was a prudent approach and plan. This also allowed me to, yet again, to stop and "smell the roses" along the way. To say we enjoyed our stay was an understatement. We had a blast.

John was an incredible host. He, along with his wife Michelle, could not have been any more hospitable. The visit was also highlighted by a cool and fun ATV adventure that John lead. During our off-road ATV adventure ride we encountered a wolf, and got to see all three of John's cabins" (that candidly, were nicer than my primary residence) and the property which provided awesome views of the area surrounding Steamboat Springs. Once we arrived back at the "cabin" we cooked pizza and shared cycling stories with hospitality that was second-to-none. When the next morning arrived, after a good night's sleep, it was time to ride again.

That next morning, we suited up for our ride and were on our way back to the Great Divide trail. This is where my two easy rest days really paid off, as I felt incredibly fresh. This was much needed too, as the next few days had us climbing from 7,000 feet to the 9,000+ range. I also knew some of the more iconic mountain passes of the Great Divide trail were on the horizon (Boreas Pass: 11,500 feet; Marshall Pass: 11,000 feet; and Indiana Pass: 12,000 feet). These worried me, as I knew anything over 9,000 feet really affected me, as altitude provides less oxygen to one's body, unless you are acclimated (which Rob and John were, given that they live in Colorado). It also did not help that they both rode lighter cyclocross bikes, which weighed nowhere near my 50-pound mountain bike behemoth, with all my gear.

Despite my trepidation, the first day with my "peloton of three" was awesome and easy. The three of us effortlessly cruised thru Lynx Pass (9,000+ feet elevation) and enjoyed more incredible Colorado views. This is where riding with others really helped, as both John and Rob provided much needed company. For riding alone is mentally challenging, especially when you do so day after day, mile after mile. It was also fun, as we would stop and chat, and just enjoyed the camaraderie of one another's company. And aside from a tough climb in the heat at the end of the day to finish in Kremling, where Rob and I would stay at a hotel (John having departed for the day, as planned), this was an easy 85-mile day.

The day was also punctuated by the funniest moment of the entire trip when we had to cross an overflowing river. John provided some incredibly funny commentary, captured on video, which we watched again and again, to non-stop laughter. In that respect, meeting people like John illustrated to me, yet again in a very personal way, why a trip like this is so special. You meet the greatest people along the way; John was one of those people. As Rob and I were at the hotel thinking through the next day's route, it became apparent that we needed to think in terms of a route adjustment, as the late May Colorado weather started to become an issue. A bad storm was on the horizon, forecasted for the next 48-hours.

At this point, I was all for making smart decisions, even if they impacted our best laid plans. In fact, most of my decisions were made to accommodate so many of the circumstances that were unique and different from others who ride the Great Divide (a world-wide pandemic, riding earlier than recommended due to the impact of weather, riding solo, riding during national racial injustice protests that erupted during my ride, etc.). This is yet another illustration of how sobriety has changed me. The old "Nate Cross" would have never shied away from danger and would have made poor decisions, without regard for the consequences.

In fact, my whole life has been marked by making poor and dangerous decisions, always without regard for others. Today, I try to make more reasoned decisions, thanks to some of the tools I have learned from my 12-Step Program. And while it may seem I am being a bit over-dramatic in this assessment, that is truly not the case -- as I continually made good (smart) decisions during the entire adventure on my second Great Divide ride -- decisions that previously I would have never considered. This is just an example of one good decision, due to the imminent poor weather.

It was in this context that it was decided Rob would call another good friend who had also planned to ride with us for a small portion of the route. His name also is Rob, and we planned to ride and stay at his place in Keystone. Ultimately, due to the storm coming in the next 48-hours, we asked Rob's friend to pick us up the next morning so we could leave from Keystone instead of arriving there the next day, as initially planned. This would allow us to beat the likely storms in the forecast, and get us to Crested Butte one day earlier. Had we not done this, we would have been certain to ride into a storm, and worse yet, ride into a mountain range with snow and during a lightning strike, which is extremely dangerous. The bottom line: we skipped a small 30-mile section of the Great Divide trail, but were smart to do so, which enabled us to ride through Boreas and Marshall Pass, which are iconic climbs along the Great Divide.

After a late morning departure from Keystone, the "two Robs" and I were on beautiful single-track through Keystone, on our way to Breckenridge, and back on the Great Divide trail for our ascent up Boreas Pass. Our eventual goal for the day was to make it to Salida, 120 miles away. All the intelligence Rob had collected about our likelihood of making it through the potentially snowy mountain pass indicated it was passable (no snow). In hindsight, if there is any one lesson learned from this journey, it is to be careful whom you get information from.

Our trip through Breckenridge was short and sweet. Once we loaded up with some food and extra water, our ascent up Boreas Pass (11,482 feet) began. Slowly but surely, we pedaled easily up this low-grade mountain. We were certain to make it through this pass without being affected by snow, as we climbed and climbed and saw no snow. That is, until we got to approximately 11,000 feet of elevation. It was at this point where I really noticed the altitude begin to affect me. My breathing became more and more difficult. I also began to labor, for no other reason other than there is less oxygen, the higher we went. At this point, snow began to appear. No big deal we thought, as we would just push our bikes through the occasional drifts on the road.

However, as we got near the top, the road became un-rideable. We needed to push our bikes through the snow unless we were to turn back. This was not an option, as we had to move forward, to finish our 120-mile day ride and most importantly, beat the storms that lay ahead. It was at this point where yet another of the other tools I have learned in my sobriety began to really help. I remember saying to myself, "This is no fun," but continually reminded myself to take it "one day at a time" and to use this moment to improve my conscious contact with God, allowing Him to give me the power to mentally get through this challenge: to get me through this day. Whether it is in cycling, or work, or sobriety -- or any other challenge in life, for that matter -- becoming God conscious and following His guidance has become an effective strategy for being able to confront and overcome any challenge.

As I reflect on my ordeal *trudging* through the snow, I am reminded that recovery is no cakewalk. It involves serious effort that requires work, not unlike this situation I found myself in. In a broader sense, it involves admitting your faults, clearing the wreckage from your past, and giving freely of others. It is the spirit of this message that helped me "*trudge the road of happy destiny*" as I worked to summit this climb.

I also used any other mental device at my disposal to confront the challenge at hand. At one point, I remember looking down at an inspirational note my daughter taped to my bike bag: "*Keep Pushing... I Love You – Nicole.*"

There was newfound humor in this message in the sense that the literal and figurative interpretation of her inspirational message now became a humorous sidebar to my act as I was literally "pushing" my bike through the snow, step by step.

But, within a short period of time, both Rob and I had pushed our way through this half-mile stretch of deep snow, where I occasionally would "post-hole" and fall through the snow, to make it to the top of Boreas Pass!

We now were able to begin to enjoy the fruits of our labor, as we prepared to descend the mountain. Unfortunately, at the top of the pass I had to change my socks, now soaked by the snow, and forgot to seal and buckle my clothing bag. Usually, no big deal, and something I never forget to do.

However, as I descended the mountain, a piece of clothing fell out and got caught in my back tire and chain. Not only did I think I had a major tire blow-out and almost crashed, but fortunately, the incident allowed me to realize that I had been dropping clothing on the descent. As I looked back up the road, my clothing littered the trail, necessitating a quick ride back up the mountain to pick up my clothing, piece by piece. It could have been worse, especially if this occurred without notice. Thankfully, I retrieved my items and continued the descent.

At this point, we had spent precious hours *trudging* through the snow, and climbing. The 120-mile day that lay ahead now seemed overwhelming, partly due to the 9,000+ altitude we were riding through, but especially now that we were in a valley. Here, you guessed it, were strong headwinds and a sandy washboard-like road. Just what I did not need, as I was tired. It was at this point where appreciation for my friend Rob became accentuated; as Rob did all he could to help and shield me from the wind, just to be there for me. This was so him, as he is one of the most caring, giving and compassionate people I have ever met, and he knew I was suffering.

Despite my fatigue, we forged ahead on this lonely wind-ridden valley road. This is where mental fatigue started to really get the best of me. I did not say anything to Rob, but as an experienced cyclist, he knew. I had now been on my journey for over a week, and while my legs were not physically tired, boredom from long stretches began to take their toll. Additionally, the barren landscape now began to test my patience. I started to question the point of seeing the same damn thing over and over; day after day; mile after mile. But, as was the case with the whole journey, whining about it gets you nowhere. Instead, we just pedaled.

I also became concerned about water and waved down a pick-up truck to see if the driver had any. Fortunately, he had a cooler on his truck, and stopped to help us by providing water. We then continued toward the South Park town of Hartsel, where we stopped to eat. This is where I truly lost my will, as the altitude made the distance traveled that day seem as though we had already ridden 120-miles, even though we had only covered 80-miles. It was late in the afternoon (4:30 p.m.) and I knew we still had about 40-miles to go and did not want to ride in the dark. At this point, while loading up on pizza to re-energize, I struck up a conversation with a local resident and asked if they were heading to Salida. While they indicated they were not headed in our direction, they knew why I was asking. Instinctively, I surrendered and asked them point-blank if they could give us a ride (or "boost" as I referred to it) up the road 20-miles, which would allow me to mentally justify a more manageable 20-mile ride into Salida. I felt as if I had given up.

However, in my mind, especially during these past four years of sobriety, I have learned that there is no shame in asking for help. In fact, that is what the whole AA Program is all about, asking for help and helping others. Given the mental state I was in, I quickly forgave myself, accepted the offer of a ride, and eliminated the need to ride late into the night. I know that I would not have been put in this position, but for dealing with all the elements on Boreas Pass, spending considerable time *trudging* through the snow. But along with the altitude, I was depleted of all my remaining energy. And, despite being mentally defeated, I would just have to make it up to myself the next day, as we had another significant mountain pass to conquer. We were also still racing the storms, which were to hit the next day. Eventually, we made it to Salida and found a hotel, after having ridden approximately 95-miles for the day, with significant climbing.

Awakening the next morning in Salida, I felt so much better. A good night's sleep and large meal had done wonders. We also figured that if we could leave early, we might be able to get the 60-mile day in before getting hit by some of the storms, which were engulfing large towns all around the area. Ultimately, we got lucky and were able to successfully climb the 11,000-foot peak of Marshall Pass, and descend into the town of Sargents, where Rob's wife Siga eventually picked us up. This also allowed us time to order and engulf a huge plate of Elk-meatloaf and mashed potatoes, which was outstanding. Within an hour, Siga picked us up and we were off to my scheduled retreat in Crested Butte, to rest for the remainder of the Memorial Day weekend at their second home, as initially planned. It also gave me a nice opportunity to visit the town, and spend time with their daughter, Sofija, one of their two children whom I loved to be around.

This scheduled stop also provided me with a nice physical break too. But candidly, I was in a dark spot, mentally. I needed to get through a self-created mental roadblock, as I still had 150-miles of Colorado riding, and at least 600-700 miles to go to Mexico. I was nowhere near being done, and that rough patch I had near Hartsel really bummed me out, as there is something about riding in altitude that just puts me in slow motion and messes with my head.

So, I took advantage of my time in Crested Butte and basically just rested and ate, as Siga and Rob were incredible hosts, always tending to my needs. I recall Rob sensing that I seemed down. For me, his instincts were spot on. And although I enjoyed this ride and my time with Rob and his friends, it seemed to me that some of the long stretches of the same landscape, that often times occur for the whole day, seemed to never end. And this was beginning to take a mental toll on me.

As I shared my fears with Rob about what lay ahead, he reminded me that "if it was easy, it would not be worth completing." This was a pretty obvious statement for me, as that was the whole point of my personal challenge to bike through Wyoming, Colorado and New Mexico -- to get to the Mexican border. But, his words of wisdom were a nice reminder, at just the right time, to help erase the seeds of doubt that were beginning to solidify in my head.

During my visit, I also had time to do something I had not previously done with anyone beyond the confines of my AA meetings: to admit and share my story of alcoholism, and why I wanted to write this book. So, after dinner that first night, I began to share my story with Rob, Siga and Sofija. In sum, our conversation resulted in affirmation that there really was no shame in admitting what they had known all too long (as they knew me well, since college); that I had a drinking problem, and that I was working daily to improve myself and my life with others. This became a more comforting experience than I initially might have thought.

During this break, I also reflected on my journey through recovery over these past four years, which reminded me of many experiences I have had that required work every day, one day at a time, to be successful, regardless of the ordeal. In that context, I began to gain some of my confidence back, and began to look forward to the next day when I would hop back on my bike, for the final push through Colorado into New Mexico.

Indeed, the very next day, a new sense of urgency and purpose to finish my ride were somehow instilled into my being. I had bid adieu to Rob, as he dropped me back on the Great Divide route near where we finished the previous few days, and I was on my way. For some reason, my whole attitude totally changed, despite the fact that I now would be on my own the rest of the way, with no further plans for rest. As I wandered through the Cochetopa Canyon on the way to my ultimate 100-mile destination for the day, to the town of Del Norte, this day's ride seemed effortless. I climbed beautifully up the two 10,000-foot climbs that needed to be tackled that day and began to enjoy the beauty of the landscape that just days ago seemed trivial and boring to me.

I also did not feel alone, as my morning prayers and God consciousness began to take on new meaning and purposeful fulfillment. Additionally, the realization that I would be crossing over into New Mexico the next day added a boost to my mental state. Only one thing stood in my way: Indiana Pass, the tallest mountain on the whole Great Divide. But, for now, the task at hand was to get through this day. My attitude became solidified, with the "one day at a time" approach serving me well. As I pulled up into Del Norte, ready to rest and recover, I was in for another surprise, stumbling upon one of my other favorite stops of the trip.

In Del Norte, I was surprised to find a bike shop that was attached to the Mellow Moon Motel, catering to cyclists on the Great Divide. I met the owner, Sam, who took care of my every need. The place was indeed geared to cyclists, which I thought was so cool. It was also nice to know that while I was showering, Sam was hard at work looking over my bike. I needed this assurance, as my brakes had not really felt right for several days. So Sam began to work on my bike to see what might be wrong. The brakes needed bleeding (air taken out of the cable) and by the next morning were fixed and now worked like new. Sam also put me in touch with a local resident who knew the trail well, and while I had heard that Indiana Pass was clear of snow, I had heard that story before, only to have to *trudge* through snow to get through. In this case, Indiana Pass was higher, and more likely to be impassable.

As expected, I was able to verify that it would be necessary to circumvent Indiana Pass, once I left the Mellow Moon Motel. Not only were there no food supply towns, but also the Skyline Lodge at the top of Indiana Pass was not open due to the pandemic. And a good ten-mile section at the top was impassable due to the snow. I was bummed about this, as I truly wanted to do all three of the big climbs in Colorado, but also wanted to do the smart and safe thing. Thus, when I left the next morning, I would have to travel around this section of the Great Divide on the road.

When morning arrived, I was fully onboard with the new plan. I was excited to be leaving Colorado and high altitude, and to be entering New Mexico. This provided a much-needed mental boost, with my destination determined to be the town of Ojo Caliente, in New Mexico. I had also decided and made plans to stay at the Taos Trail Inn, which had not had a guest for over two months but was now open and willing to provide me with a room, and was an incredibly unique place to stay. With a decision made, the plan called for a 110-mile day, which would put me back on the Great Divide trail the very next day. I was also comforted by the fact that this new route would include some unique towns, which also provided water and food along the way.

It was at this point that I started to come to terms with my route diversions and was okay about it. It was no longer a fixation to ride solely *on the Great Divide trail*, so long as the bigger picture would be addressed: being safe and making it to Mexico, given that I was alone and entering New Mexico, the final state on this journey. An additional challenge became apparent as well, as it became real necessary to focus on staying hydrated and cool, given the increasing heat index and obvious limited water availability.

The next morning, after a quick breakfast, I rode headed for the New Mexico border, and Ojo Caliente, for the 110-mile ride through the Carson National Forest. After a few hours riding, I arrived in the town of Antonito, riding down State Route 285. This also marked the half-way mark for my day's ride. Antonito was my last town in Colorado, before I hit the New Mexico border. After another quick meal, I was back on the bike headed for the state border, and stopped for what was now my mandatory "Welcome" sign photo-op. This provided a huge boost to my morale. Then, after a few selfies, I was on my way with approximately 50 long, hot miles to go, to reach Ojo Caliente, now finally in New Mexico.

Continuing toward my daily destination, I got lucky again by avoiding an afternoon thunderstorm. Riding alongside a storm cloud that continually cast a dark shadow on the road, it seemed as if it was going to "dump on me" at any minute. Fortunately, this outcome was somehow avoided. Additionally, along the way I found all kinds of ionic places to stop for snacks and a few cokes, and to stock up on water, to continue the ride into Ojo Caliente to the Taos Trail Inn.

Not long after crossing the border into New Mexico, it became obvious from my first destination that the *look and feel of everything* began to appear so much different from all the towns I had experienced thus far. The dwellings, towns and buildings along the way reminded me of Mexico and were so much different from everything I saw just that morning in Del Norte. What a difference a day makes!

CHAPTER SIX

2020 Great Divide Ride

New Mexico: Heat Advisory & No Water!

From the Colorado Border to the USA/Mexico Border!
Approximately 576-miles (19,453 feet of climbing)

The day began like most others. However, this day was much better than most, as I had crossed the border into New Mexico the previous day, and now was in my third and final state! Though, it started like most others: I would get up, eat what I had on me, or visit a restaurant if one was open, and plan my route around finding food along the way.

On this particular day, I woke up in Ojo Caliente, where I spent an unusual night watching Jimmy Stewart's Christmas Classic

"It's a Wonderful Life." This could not have been more inappropriate for the time of year, but there was no working cable TV in the room, but instead only a DVD player with just one DVD. Worked for me! This unique situation was par for the course on this journey, and this hotel was as unique as the town. I had also enjoyed Mexican food again the night before, at the only restaurant or food option in town -- due to Covid-19. At this point, I was pretty used to this scenario, as the pandemic clearly had an impact on my ride.

Upon leaving Ojo Caliente, I was in pretty good spirits. I left early for my first full-day riding in New Mexico, with a plan to complete 95-miles to end up in the town of Cuba. Leaving town, I found myself in a beautiful canyon climbing out of the valley I had previously descended into the previous day. It was beautiful. It was not long until I entered the town of El Rito, and was back on the Great Divide trail.

In this town, the most unusual sight appeared, as a local resident had constructed a "Mars Polar Lander" in their front yard. This object can best be described an 80-foot tall clock tower, with every item the artist could find in his back-yard attached to it. As they say, a picture is worth a thousand words. Your guess is as good as mine, in terms of what it was?

Within a short period of time, I easily rode into the town of Abiquiu, where I loaded up with water, as the next 65-mile section of the Great Divide went deep into the desert and mountains. Heat, dehydration and personal safety started to become a concern.

Had I been in the Tour Divide race, I certainly would not have diverted to the road around this section of the Great Divide trail. However, as was the case during my entire journey, *this was my ride*. I had promised my wife and family I would be safe and make good decisions. The heat was a serious and significant issue given that an "Extreme Heat Alert" had been issued for the areas into which I was riding. It was now routinely over 100-degrees by 2:00 p.m. every day, so I decided to divert to the road, along State Route 96 into Cuba. This decision was not just smart, but allowed me to see interesting things which would not have been as accessible on the Great Divide trail. And besides, at this point in the journey, it was not as if I had not seen enough of desert, sand, bumpy roads and rocks.

Subsequently, my ride from Abiquiu to Cuba was incredibly eventful. At one point, I stopped by one of the many roadside memorials punctuating the way, but this one was different from most. I was now going in and out of Indian Reservations. Much to my surprise, the Native Americans apparently buried victims of traffic fatalities right alongside the road. This became obvious, as the memorial was not just a tribute with a cross and flowers, but rather an actual tomb. This roadside tomb and vault even had solar lighting, and an elaborate spread of flowers and signage, which caught my attention, to say the least.

As I continued to ride and periodically stop to cool down in sporadic and infrequent shady spots, I also stopped in the towns of Youngsville, Coyote, Gallina and Regina to get water, and at one point, an ice cream cone! To me, this was not only a way to reward myself, but also serve as a purposeful reminder to never forget to "stop and smell the roses" along the way and enjoy oneself.

In my mind, there is no better way to enjoy oneself than to have a vanilla ice-cream cone. In doing so, it became apparent that I was clearly enjoying the opportunity to ride through towns, as opposed to riding in the remote desert; as I loved to meet people and see how others live, in this part of our country.

As the day wore on, I made additional stops at historic markers along the way. One stop was an old 1946 fire engine. By early afternoon, I was rolling into the town of Cuba, headed for The Cuban Motel, another of the many low-cost hotels (less than $45) along the Great Divide. The affable inn keeper was as entertaining as she was gracious. Yet again, I settled into my room, showered, did some laundry by hand, and strategized as to what feast awaited me, as riding all day sure worked up an appetite. It was also nice to be able to turn on the air conditioning in the room, as the heat was increasing with each southern mile gained.

In that respect, I began to look at the forecast for the rest of the journey. My worst fears were realized, as previously mentioned: I was heading into an extreme heat alert -- with temperatures forecast in the 100-115 degrees range! More than ever, I became very determined to finish this ride, before I melted. This also meant a more concerted effort to leave very early in the morning, each day until the finish, as the afternoon sun sucked every ounce of energy from one's body. *That is exactly what I did the next day, which turned out to be the most memorable and meaningful day of the entire adventure.*

Leaving the town of Cuba at 5:45 a.m., I had a 120-mile ride to reach the large town of Grants. This section of the Great Divide followed along a flat section of road, further into some of the many Indian Reservations in that section of the state, including Navajo Nation.

It certainly was not lost on me either that all the Indian Territories had been hit hard by Covid-19, late in the pandemic, especially the Navajo Nation. For that reason, I wanted to be as respectful as I could with the wishes of the local citizenry, by being especially mindful to wear a mask; which I did whenever interacting with anyone along the journey.

On this particular day, I would be stopping for water and food at both of the two convenience stores that existed along the route. And when I stopped at each, it was obvious to see these stores took the Covid-19 issue very seriously, as illustrated by the incredibly strong smell of bleach when entering each store. Yet again, I felt safe.

As the miles clicked by easily, helped by a strong tailwind at my back, I rode through a patchwork of several different Indian territories and was continually struck by the beauty of the landscape, contrasted by the noticeable poverty of the area. I found this somewhat disturbing, along with the dismay I felt as I saw the whole stretch of road littered with trash and an occasional illegal dump of everything from toilets to dressers and tires. Indeed, it was an odd scene of contrasts.

However, what was most striking, and memorable, was a sign I saw that really hit a nerve. This was approximately halfway through my ride, having now clicked off 60-miles on this day.

This sign had a huge impact on me. While I do not consider myself to be spiritually deficient, nor do I view myself as a religious zealot, it just seemed odd to me that this sign was along the road, right in the middle of nowhere. A sign like this, in the middle of nowhere, has IMPACT.

And when you ride, you have nothing to do but think. Whether you are listening to tunes on your playlist, or just daydreaming, a sign like this grabs your attention. For me, this sign had an impact, a huge one on my psyche.

I continued to pedal, while at the same time counting my blessings, as I did each day. However, this sign, both literally and figuratively, put me in a serene and spiritual frame of mind. More so than I would have ever thought.

For hours, I thought about everything I had gone through, not just on this journey, but over the course of the past four years, since I have led a sober life. I truly have God to thank for my recovery, and my new lease on life since I have learned to live each day, one day at a time.

I also have come to realize that every day is a blessing and a gift. Since this realization, I could not be more thankful for everything in my life that has improved. In that respect, I started to gain a new sense of purpose for *why I did this ride in the first place*, ever since people repeatedly asked me this same question. This is a fair question, as I asked this of myself each day of the ride, and especially when I began to think of quitting, which occurred frequently and every single day. If I ever had a spiritual moment or moment of clarity on this ride -- this was it.

As I continued to spend the next few hours thinking about how fortunate I was to have been brought up with strong values, and the impact of Catholic upbringing, I continued to pedal. All the while, the heat intensified. Again, there was no shade anywhere, and although I was now approximately 95-miles into my 120-mile day, I needed a rest in the shade.

This is also where I experienced the greatest epiphany during my entire trip, and my entire journey in recovery.

The temperature was now over 100-degrees, and it was past 1:00 p.m., with the hottest part of the day yet to come. With no shade ahead, the next 25-miles to Grants was going to be a struggle. It was at this point a pick-up truck appeared on the horizon. For me, as I look back retrospectively, this was no ordinary pick-up truck, nor was the driver an ordinary local resident along the road. This was a gift from God -- not only in the sense that the driver was a kind soul willing to share some relevant information, and eventually offer me a ride into town -- but because of who he was, with a message that resonated with me, to this day.

The driver slowed and asked if I was okay. I was fine, had enough water and would be okay. But he shared that I was now in Navajo Nation, during a lockdown that began at noon, with serious fines of $1,000 if caught. He explained that he was headed out of the area and was willing to throw my bike in the back of his pick-up truck if I wanted. It did not take much convincing, especially after he pointed out that I "stuck out like a sore thumb" and was sure to get fined; and reminded me that they were not messing around. That was all I needed to hear.

Loading my bike into his truck and putting my mask on to be respectful of his wishes, this is where an odd sense of familiarity came over me. I felt so comfortable with my newfound friend, whose name was Derek. Immediately, we chatted about everything, but it was not long before he did something that caught my attention. Derek reached down below the ignition and blew into the straw of an ignition interlock breathalyzer, which is a device connected to a vehicle to determine one's blood alcohol concentration. As Derek did this, he began to explain that he is an alcoholic, with 12-years of sobriety and (aside from a few relapses) began to explain the impact alcohol has had on his life. I quickly pointed out my shared experience. To say the least, he had a very active listener; all while getting me out of a potential $1,000 fine for violating a pandemic lockdown that went until Sunday evening, while also saving me from the afternoon heat.

It was at this point that Derek began to tell HIS STORY, which ultimately was MY STORY. It was all too familiar to me over the course of the past 35-years since I began my weekend drinking binges. *With each word he uttered, I could not believe how similar his situation was to mine.* He told me about how he abused alcohol when he was young, eventually developing a pattern of weekend alcohol abuse, if for no other reason than to just get trashed. He shared how his actions created hardship on his family, both financially and legally, and how consequences from his actions caused great pain for him and his loved ones as well. He told me about what a terrible husband he was, because of his desire to choose alcohol over everything else in his life, just so he could numb his pain. He shared his anger from being a child from a divorced family, and his lack of devotion to his faith. He talked about all the misguided anger he possessed, and how that was the root of his problems, which he tried to erase by drinking, all to numb his pain. And he talked about his resentments, and how he began to understand, only after getting serious about his disease through his involvement with the AA Program, how this had changed his life.

For me, this moment was so incredibly meaningful. Not just because I had seen that "Jesus sign" earlier in my ride and was in a spiritually reflective mood; nor because I was just given a ride, but rather because it presented an unique opportunity to be reminded by someone else just like me, that life is better sober. This timely reminder also reinforced my belief that I can enjoy life "one day at a time" without alcohol.

Since I had been searching my soul on the bike over the course of the past two weeks, this exchange with Derek was more than mere coincidence. *For me, this was a message that was heaven sent.* It also reaffirmed my belief that when a coincidence occurs, it is God's way of blinking, to remind us He is with us, looking out for us. On this day, He sure was looking out for me.

After this special moment of revelation, Derek and I arrived in Grants. I thanked him not only for the ride, but also for his candor and sharing his personal experience with me. I could not have been more sincere, as my encounter with Derek had a *profound* effect on me. Within minutes, I was off through the town of Grants, determined to find a hotel to share my story with my wife, Rose. Having checked into my room, I immediately called Rose.

Calling Rose daily was customary if I had cell reception, or at least to contact her by text when I arrived at my daily destination, as she worried about me (especially when alone) during this whole trip. Though, this call was different. When the phone rang, she answered and had just awakened from a nap. I asked her if she had a moment, so I could share a story.

I then began to explain the impact the "Jesus" sign had on me, and how my whole day had been fixated trying to figure out some spiritual purpose behind its placement. I then went further and shared my interaction with Derek, and what he had shared with me. It is important to note that Rose not only has had to deal with me for the past 24 years in marriage, but she has been at "ground zero" and witness to, and the direct recipient of, all my actions and past boorish behavior, as a result of drinking. This is a complicated and complex set of circumstances to explain. But suffice it to say, earlier in my recovery when it came time for me to make amends for all my actions, as suggested in the 12-Step Program, I really never did justice to Rose, nor give her an apology worthy of what Rose fairly deserved.

Now I began to cry, admitting that she not only deserved a more sincere apology for my past actions as a result of drinking over the years; but that like Derek, I was a terrible husband when drinking, and sincerely apologized: for the anger; for the irritability that results from drinking; for the constant reliance on her when I needed a ride from being drunk; for the embarrassing situations I had put her through from drinking too much; for my insensitivity; for the harm I caused to others; and for just being "Drunk Boy."

Sadly, the list goes on, and on. At this point, she started to cry too. This became a special moment: one that was long overdue.

At the end of the call, Rose thanked me for sharing my story, and like me, wondered aloud that there might be some good that comes from this ride, after all. This was a heartfelt moment for both of us.

I rested comfortably on my hotel bed for a few moments. Within a few minutes, I received a text from Rose. She clearly was as moved by the moment we just shared:

Thank you for your call & sharing with me your thoughts & experiences. It truly touched my heart to hear those words from your heart. I am so relieved that you are safe (for now) & please continue on your journey knowing that God is always there and sends you people that will steer you in the right direction, and that will stick by you through the good and the bad. There are paths we can choose and we both have chosen paths that have been challenging. We both could have chosen an easier path, but the paths we chose shows just how strong we are individually and how to persevere. Whenever I have felt defeated and was close to throwing in the towel, I thought back to 25-years ago to the man I married. I think of the man that had tears in his eyes as I walked down the aisle to him; to the times when our friends criticized how were always holding hands; to the times we always talked to each other without walking away, etc. I knew this guy was still in there somewhere and I would wait for the day he would come back to me. I think today was the day ☺. I hope to build on this and to be able to talk more. In the words of Elton John, "Sorry seems to be the hardest word," but it is a word that brings such comfort. It does not have to mean that you are wrong, but that you just want to comfort the one you love.

I love you Nate – always have and always will. Being a good wife and mother is my dream come true. Get some rest, stay safe and give me an update on your timeline and stops. Xoxoxo – Rose.

As the day concluded, I had found special meaningful purpose for my ride on the Great Divide. From this point forward, I vowed to continue to take every day, one day at a time; treat every day as a gift; and find satisfaction in knowing that God has a plan. For me, I would have thought I did not need to be reminded of this. That was the beauty of this ride, as it served as a reminder to me that *God has a plan!* Fortunately for me, His plan involves me on a bike!

I woke the next day exhilarated. I kept thinking about what a meaningful and memorable day I had just had. But, as is the case with this journey, it was time to move on, with the realization that I did not have that far to go to the Mexican border. As in the past, I just needed to take this one day at a time, and today, my goal was to make it to Pie-Town, a town aptly named for the residents' love of pies (the town incorporated after petitioning the state to name itself based on its historical love for pies, dating to the early 1900's), and an easy 80-mile ride.

And while I was not sure if the infamous pie shops in Pie-Town would be open due to the pandemic, it certainly was on my mind all day long, especially in terms of my desire for a banana cream pie. I could not stop thinking about an edible reward at the end of the day.

There also was another reward on the horizon, as I was to ride through and experience the beauty of the El Malpaias National Park, complete with canyons and rock formations, which were some of the most magnificent of the whole ride.

As I left the El Malpaias Natonal Park, the sun began to really take its toll. Fortunately, I had left the town of Grants early enough to beat most of the heat, but it was still HOT. I was also blessed having most of the early morning portion of the ride being on the road surface, which was much easier to pedal on. And it was much faster, until approximately half-way through the ride, when I was dumped onto another sandy, bumpy "washboard" gravel road, until reaching Pie-Town.

However, this did not seem to bother me as much anymore. While I am not sure if this newfound attitude was the net result of the previous day's ride, or the fact that I was getting close to my finish at the border of Mexico, it was beginning to sink in that I now only had approximately 226-miles to go, after today's ride. Clearly, progress had been made.

Though, I still had to finish the day's ride. With about 20-miles to go until Pie-Town, I was low on water. I looked at my map and estimated there would be a well ahead. Instead, I ran into a cemetery with lots of shade, and decided to stop. This became a wise decision. However, this was no ordinary cemetery, but a small family cemetery dating back to the 1930's, with some descendants born in 1898. Pretty historic stuff.

Then, to my surprise, I noticed about twelve one-gallon jugs of water placed under a tree. This was not just a beautiful welcome site, but epitomized what the Great Divide trail is all about: strangers performing random acts of kindness for strangers like me. That is what makes this ride and my adventure so special: caring random acts like this, by anonymous trail angels, which serve as a reminder that kind people exist and are and are all around. I was so grateful.

After filling my bottles and making my way to finish the final 20-miles for the day, the most disappointing news awaited as I rode into town. Much to my dismay, I soon realized that both pie shops in town were closed. I was so bummed! This was devasting, as I thought of nothing else than Banana Cream Pie for hours.

However, the blow of this traumatic experience was quickly softened by some good news, as I stumbled upon one of the most iconic stops along the Great Divide trail: The Toaster House.

The Toaster House is no ordinary house. It is a free, donation-only hostel for hikers and bikers along the Great Divide trail, where guests can eat, sleep and socialize. Humorously, the name of the place is the result of the purposeful placement of hundreds  of broken toasters that have been hung on the gate and all over the property. Literally, there are hundreds of toasters all over the place! And, once you go inside there are so many other knick-knacks all over the place, it becomes the ultimate but overwhelming sensory experience.

Additionally, people from all over the country and world stay at the Toaster House, including the day I visited, as I met people from a variety of states, and countries like New Zealand and Australia. This became an extremely fun experience, as each of us sat around sharing stories of our adventures. Had it not been for the fact that my plans were to divert off course that night so I could end up in the town of Reserve the next morning, I would have stayed the night. Regardless, I ended up staying for five to six hours, while enjoying the raucous environment and infectious spirit of this Great Divide gem along the route.

Plans for a ride to a particular hotel that night in Reserve had been coordinated to enable me to wake and ride through some towns on the way to Silver City, with a more manageable 110-mile ride the next day. As was the case with my whole journey, my diversion had a purpose -- to be safe. And with an extreme heat advisory now in effect, with temperatures expected to be above 110-degrees, and forecasted in the 115-120 degree range by early afternoon, this spelled disaster. I certainly did not think it was a good idea to be on this specific section of the Great Divide trail, as this was a section with very limited water. In sum, had it not been so hot, I likely would not have diverted. But, I also wanted to divert to do the 110-mile road ride the next day that would route me through the Gila National Forest, which I had heard was beautiful. Additionally, I also felt that at this point, I had seen my fair share of New Mexico desert, sand, rock, and sagebrush.

Fear of the heat was not unfounded, being heightened by a phone call with Jeff Sharpe, who was my southernmost contact at the end of my ride. We had arranged for him to pick me up when I hit the Mexico border. Jeff had joked that I could not have picked a worse week to finish the Great Divide, given the worsening heat situation that was to occur over the next week. His point was not lost on me, which served as another reason to just FINISH this ride, quickly.

Mentally too, I was ready to finish, and any further delays would put me in a much worse heat scenario. Thus, I was now determined to finish as quickly as possible. Obtaining a ride from personnel of the Frisco Inn Hotel, to my room in the town of Reserve, ultimately saved another day too of melting in the desert of New Mexico, with little water. So, with the decision made, I ended up in the town of Reserve, after an eventful and entertaining ride with the son of the hotel owner, driving into Reserve from Pie-Town.

When I woke early the next morning to get a jump on the mid-day heat, I was so pleased with my decision, as the ride took me up another beautiful canyon into the Gila National Forest.

After an awesome and much needed breakfast, I was on my way with a few climbs, followed by some fun descents. The scenery was magnificent, and I was able to stop along the way at some roadside gas stations, where I loaded up with water (and had yet another vanilla ice cream cone…) for the final long climb up into the town of Silver City.

Like most days with the intense heat, it was necessary to stop periodically to try to cool down in whatever sporadic shade could be found along the way. At one point, while cooling down, I even had time to call my brother David, as I found it humorous that he had just texted asking how things were going, and I felt obligated to call him with a candid assessment: that I was on the side of the road, hiding from the sun, while trying to avoid rattlesnakes. Such is life on the Great Divide.

It also did not help riding into a headwind, but for some reason it did not seem to bother me as much as usual, because it was starting to really sink in that after today's ride, I only had 126-miles to go! This alone motivated me, and within time, despite having to ride throughout the mid-day sun, I arrived at the town of Silver City. I was so grateful, as the ride took its toll on me, but within a short period of time, was in a hotel room by 5:00 p.m. Though, I started to smell the finish, and my ultimate destination of Mexico!

In that respect, Silver City meant so much to me, not only because it is a bigger town with many options for food, but because it represented the last big town I would stay in until the finish. From here, it was just an 80-mile ride into the town of Hachita, and then the last mad-dash to the finish at the Mexican border, on a flat 46-mile road.

When I awakened, I decided I would only ride 80-miles the next day and would save the final "46-mile stretch" until the following morning. All of this was in the interest of being smart, by staying out of the mid-day heat, which I had now had enough of. Again, I cannot emphasize enough the impact the heat has on the body: it truly sucks every ounce of energy out of you, and I wanted to finish on a high note, so I could truly enjoy the final miles when it was not so hot. This decision also gave me an opportunity to spend the afternoon of the next day at *The Bike Ranch* in Hachita, and allowed me to "hang-out" with Jeff Sharpe, who is a local cycling legend on the Great Divide trail. This is exactly what I did. I had a blast.

As an aside, I would be remiss not to speak further about Jeff without telling you a little bit more about him, as he epitomizes everything good about the Great Divide. Jeff is known by everyone along the entire route and is known to be one of the most genuine, giving people along the trail. In my case, I had contacted Jeff weeks before my ride, to coordinate a ride from the finish, to Tuscon, Arizona. This included picking me up after the final 46-mile stretch, at the Mexico border. After I was done with my Great Divide adventure, I would meet and stay for a while with my sister Dana, who lives in Phoenix.

In sum, this is what Jeff Sharp does for his livelihood, but he does so much more. Aside from all the community work in Hachita that he performs for the local Community Center, his home has become *The Bike Ranch* because of all the assistance he provides to cyclists from around the world, all year round. This is the type of subculture that exists on the Great Divide, that you never really know about unless you experience it. For me, this is what my ride was all about -- meeting great people like Jeff Sharp.

Further, whether it is food, clothing or a ride -- Jeff never hesitates to help. During the Tour Divide race, when riders are finishing daily, he constantly drives back and forth to the border, picking up riders, and shuttles them to wherever they need to go, to catch a bus or plane, regardless of the distance or inconvenience. Again, Jeff epitomizes the type of giving person you will always find along the route, which is why the term "trail angel" exists. In my mind, Jeff is more than just a "trail angel." He was just a good dude, and I really enjoyed meeting him!

However, it was now time to finish my penultimate ride, an 80-mile journey from Silver City into Hachita, which became one of my easier and more enjoyable rides. This ride was somewhat uneventful as well, which allowed me to ride the roads for about 25-miles out of Silver City, until I dropped onto the final desert section of the Great Divide trail. This turned out to be a fun, rolling 40-mile gravel section, which I was able to complete by around 11:30 a.m. Once out of this section, I rolled into a unique town with a visit to the "Continental Divide Historic Trading Post" where I picked up a cool souvenir shirt commemorating the ride, and a few cokes and candy bars. At this point, I was feeling pretty good, with only 25-miles into Hachita, and an expected finish time of 1:30 p.m.

Candidly, at this point, I thought seriously about just finishing the whole journey, as the final 46-miles would be quick and easy. However, because of the mid-day heat (all on black-top road, which magnifies the heat), I decided to continue to play it smart, and just finish the next morning when I would enjoy my final miles much more. Sure, this was my plan all along, but when you get that close, it sure was tempting to just "get it done." Thus, I exercised my better judgement and upon riding into Hachita, contacted Jeff and relaxed the whole rest of the day as planned.

However, I did end up helping Jeff paint his ceiling. As odd as this sounds, this allowed me to do something for other cyclists that would come after me. It also served as an act of community service to illustrate not only my appreciation to Jeff, but an important actionable principle of my recovery program, which is to help others.

When I finally went to bed that evening, after watching on television some of the racial injustice protests that had been breaking out nationally during the last week of the ride (as if a pandemic wasn't enough...), I slept well, knowing I was almost done! Tomorrow would be a fun ride, whereby I could finally take care of my "unfinished business."

The next morning, I could not have been more excited, as it is difficult to put into words my emotion knowing my journey was almost at an end. I had been thinking about this moment for weeks, since dropping out of the Tour Divide race the previous year. In that respect, this was a moment of fulfilment.

Though, I still had 46-miles to go, and the sun was starting to crank out its daily punishment of heat.

Of all things, my tire was almost out of air. Just my luck, as I had not really had a significant mechanical issue during the whole ride. For that matter, I never really had to endure any period of rain too, which is unheard of. Regardless, I filled the tire with air and was on my way, knowing full well I could patch it if I got a flat, but what an awful way to end my journey. Within a short period of time, I began to see numerous border patrol agents, which gave me a sense of safety and comfort. I also brought out my headphones, to enjoy some favorite tunes, as I knew this final ride to the Mexican border (which incidentally was not open due to the pandemic and subsequent border closing) would be my most enjoyable ride.

Within just a short period of time, I was about 15-miles from the border. Suddenly, the signs to Antelope Wells (the border crossing) began to appear with regularity. I also saw the first rattlesnake of my trip, and even stopped to take a photo. Everything was perfect.

However, in the distance, with about 13-miles to go, a utility truck going the opposite direction slowed down and yelled something out the window. I did not hear him, nor turn around to ride up to him to hear what he was telling me. From my perspective, he was cheering me on! What a great guy I thought, and how wonderful of him to be so supportive! In retrospect, that is not what he was doing, as I was soon to learn. As I got down to an area near the 12-mile mark, the sagebrush came closer to the road. Up until now, the area in which I was biking was vast and open. Not this section. Within a few moments, I noticed a man of Mexican descent come out from the bushes. Because I was traveling at a rate of at least 20+mph, I passed him.

Immediately, I looked-back and the man was waving me to turn around and come back to him. I quickly calculated this would not be a good idea. And instinctively, I put my phone and wallet in my back-jersey pocket, so that if he or someone else got my bike, all they would get is a beat-up mountain bike and dirty laundry. Now on edge, I was constantly looking for a border agent to report this incident of a potential "guest worker" or illegal who had snuck across the border. Unfortunately, I never did see another border agent, which was odd, given that I saw plenty the first 30-miles of this 46-mile final day ride.

So, I focused on the task at hand, to finish my Great Divide ride. Within what seemed like minutes, the U.S. Customs Border Crossing was within sight, at the United States and Mexico border. This was reinforced by that beautiful sign I saw that read: "Mexico United States Boundary – 2 Miles."

It was at this point I began to cry, once again. This was another moment on the ride in which the emotion of the moment got the best of me. I had trained so hard to get to this point, and after having been defeated in sickness by the Tour Divide, I was almost there. I also thought of Rose and my two children, Jonathan and Nicole; my brother John Paul who had passed-away from cancer just 2-months earlier; and of my journey this past four years fighting the urge to drown my sorrows in beer. This truly was a wonderful moment, as I rode into the border crossing at Mexico.

My journey was complete, and my "business on the Great Divide" was indeed finished. However, the adventure was not over. As I finished, I did all the requisite things one does when finishing a ride like this. I took photos of myself and my bike in front of the border sign; I took video of the moment (including a cool dance video that is featured along with my video diary of the ride on *youtube.* To view go to: <u>Nates 2020 Ride</u>); and sent a few texts to tell people I had made it. I had completed my journey on the Great Divide!

Additionally, as an interesting aside, because my ride was being tracked (via satellite on trackleader.com), many texts hit my phone the moment I finished, as friends and family were following my ride, with every stroke of the pedal. Right then, with perfect timing, Jeff then pulled up. He was a sight for sore eyes, as I was ready to load my bike and shower. I was done.

I immediately told Jeff my story about the man at the 12-mile mark; and also told a few construction workers (who incidentally were in the vicinity at the border doing engineering work on "The Wall"), who had contacted Border Patrol. We were both interested to go by that same spot as we headed back to the *Bike Ranch* to see if a search was going on. Indeed, there was a full range of activity in that area.

As we drove up to the 12-mile mark, on my return trip in Jeff's car, a Border Patrol helicopter was hovering close to the ground. A few other Border Patrol agents were also on the ground. As we approached, Jeff rolled down the window and informed the agent that I was the person who spotted the man. After I gave a brief description of the man and told my story, we drove off as the agent told us they had discovered his tracks and assured us this person would be apprehended. Nothing like an international incident at the border, while finishing my "bucket list" ride on the Great Divide!

My journey was now truly complete. I then went back to the *Bike Ranch* and showered for my trip to Tuscon with Jeff, where I would meet my sister, Dana. My ride was now officially over. What a day. What a journey. What an accomplishment. What an adventure!

Once I settled later that day, I posted this summary on *facebook* along with the photo of myself (previous page) holding up my bike (a common standard photo of Great Divide riders):

After a little over two weeks of riding, I am happy to report that I took care of some "unfinished business" on & along the Great (Continental) Divide! My 1,700-mile journey thru Wyoming, Colorado & New Mexico was incredible, to say the least, and allowed me to meet so many inspiring people along the way, as I arrived at the Mexico/USA border this morning in Antelope Wells, NM. Look forward to sharing some of my stories (soon) about riding cross country during a pandemic; biking thru a Navajo Nation lock-down; riding thru the Great Basin; biking while racial injustice protests erupted across the country; dodging rattlesnakes, bears, antelopes, elk, wild horses & many other wildlife; and an international incident 12-miles from the border when an illegal jumped out of the bushes in an apparent attempt to snag me and my bike. Many other stories to follow, soon. Thank you to all that were so supportive!

I was so happy to be done! Shortly I arrived at my sister's house in Scottsdale, AZ. I was able to take advantage of a 10-day period to rest, relax and to go back to remote work, while basking in the glory knowing that I was able to take care of my **UNFINISHED BUSINESS** on the **GREAT DIVIDE**, *ONE DAY AT A TIME!*

REFLECTIONS

"God, grant me the *SERENITY*
to accept the things I cannot change;
COURAGE to change the things I can;
and *WISDOM* to know the difference."

Reinhold Niebuhr

The Serenity prayer (above) is a prayer I often recite as I live *one day at a time*. As I reflect on my second attempt to take care of some "unfinished business" by completing my Great Divide ride, this prayer became invaluable. It also applies to every aspect of my life, a critical lesson that was driven home to me by what I learned about myself on the ride:

I have learned that every day is a gift,
and that God Has A Plan.

This lesson has become my mantra. It has also become the foundation of my current mindset. In that respect, I have come to realize that God is doing for us what we could not do for ourselves. This realization has allowed me to open my eyes and ask for help when needed, and to make amends to those I have harmed, which has further strengthened my resolve relative to the significance and importance of helping others. This is the single most important foundational principle of the AA program.

This new mindset prepared me for this ride during a worldwide pandemic, as one of the most important things I have also learned in sobriety is that by living life *one day at a time*, I am more able to be flexible, so I can deal with each situation life throws at me, without becoming too overwhelmed.

Specifically, with the arrival of Covid-19, the pandemic which affected not just me but everyone else worldwide, this was an attitude we all learned to adapt to as we have come to accept our "new normal." This is the mindset that not only helps me in all my endeavors, whether it is personal or professional, but foremost with my sobriety. One thing for sure: I learned so much about myself during MY JOURNEY, and had a great time. I also met some incredible people and saw some incredible places during my adventure.

I also learned how to just enjoy myself. On several occasions throughout this book, I mentioned that I wanted this second attempt at the Great Divide to be a chance to not be as concerned with "racing" or be too focused on "logging endless miles" each day; but instead to learn how to allow myself to stop along the way to "smell the roses." I certainly did this, which made for such an incredibly rich experience.

My journey also reinforced the principle that although I may possess the right attitude and be on the right path in terms of sobriety, unless I approach sobriety *one day at a time,* all my sobriety progress can come to an immediate halt!

Additionally, my journey taught me I still need to stay focused to improve upon dealing with all my shortcomings and imperfections. In that respect, I still have a long way to go. I will never be perfect and will always need to continue to work daily, once day at a time, to focus on striving to be a better person.

This begins with being honest with myself. That is what I tried to do while sharing my story, in a brutally honest manner, as my ultimate hope is that I can convey to others that the disease of alcoholism, or any other form of addiction, is not something we should be afraid to discuss.

It is my hope others will not look upon my imperfections in a negative light either, as I have made mistakes, but am trying to become a better person as a result.

Only when we begin to have a candid conversation about alcoholism can we begin to help *erase the stigma associated with addiction* to help provide resources to people struggling with these types of diseases, as well as to the families and loved ones of those struggling alongside them.

"Chaos, uncertainty, doubt, and insecurity can cause us to re-enter dynamics that are unhealthy and dysfunctional. Remember your boundaries, tap into your worth, and keep choosing your healing over what might be familiar."

Vienna Pharaon

APPENDICES

Appendix 1. About the Author: Nate Cross

Appendix 2. About the Editor: James Mayer

Appendix 3. About the "Foreward" Author: Konan Stephens

Appendix 4. Recovery: The 12 Steps of AA

Appendix 5. Recovery: The 12 Promises of AA

Appendix 6. Great Divide Bike-Packing List

Appendix 1

About the Author: Nate Cross

Nate Cross lives in Cleveland, Ohio, and is a graduate of Cleveland State University, where he received his Bachelor's Degree (BA) in 1987 and Master's Degree in Public Administration (MPA) in 1989. His professional career began in 1990 while serving as the Marketing & Special Event Coordinator for the National Multiple Sclerosis (MS) Society, where he managed several national events and campaigns.

After several years at The MS Society, Nate worked in the political world for several elected officials, including Lieutenant Governor Mike DeWine (now currently Governor of Ohio); and Congressman Martin Hoke, which eventually lead to his role as the initial Executive Director of Downtown Development Coordinators (later renamed Downtown Cleveland Partnership; then Downtown Cleveland Alliance). This new group of downtown stakeholders was created by Cleveland Mayor Michael R. White and Albert Ratner of Forest City Enterprises, and chaired by retired Federal Judge Alvin (Buddy) Krenzler. Its primary focus was the development of several projects relative to the opening of the Gateway Stadiums (Progressive Field and Rocket Mortgage Fieldhouse).

Once the Gateway Stadiums opened to the public, Judge Krenzler introduced and encouraged Nate to join the staff of Cuyahoga County Commissioner Lee Weingart, where he was appointed Chief Administrative Aide. After Mr. Weingart's subsequent election loss two years later, Nate was hired by

Richard J. Fasenmyer, Chairman/CEO of RJF International Corporation, where he served as Executive Director for The RJF Foundation, a private foundation located in Akron, Ohio. In this role, Nate managed an effort to raise funds to endow a research chair in clinical immunology at The Cleveland Clinic Foundation, coordinating black-tie dinners across the country.

At the completion of this project, Nate then made a conscious decision to re-focus and utilize his fundraising and management skills, when he became Executive Director of the Northern Ohio Chapter of the Leukemia & Lymphoma Society, serving in this role for 6-years, until 2005. Subsequently, he joined the staff at University Hospitals in Cleveland to work on a capital campaign for the new Seidman Cancer Center. In 2007, Nate then became the Executive Director for the Northern Ohio Chapter of the Cystic Fibrosis Foundation, where he has served in this capacity since 2007.

PERSONAL: Nate became involved in fundraising while in college on a "whim" while conceiving, creating, organizing and participating in several events for his fraternity that landed him in the Guinness Book of World Records.

The events were a *53-day Trampoline Marathon* (in 1985); and a *600-Mile Bathtub Push* (in 1986, Cleveland to New York City) to raise funds for St. Jude Children's Research Hospital.

He also organized and participated in a **400-mile keg-roll** from Washington D.C., to Cleveland (first photo); and a national **1600-mile keg-roll** (second photo) from Boston (MA) to Orlando (FL), also as fundraisers for St. Jude's Children's Research Hospital, which ultimately led him to his interest in fundraising and non-profit management.

In a volunteer capacity, Nate has also been elected to public office, where he served one-term on the

Westlake School Board, from 2010-2013. He was also a public official as a member of the Westlake City Planning Commission; served as a member of the Westlake Board of Education Vision 2020 Committee; and was Co-Chair of the Crocker Park Citizens Advisory Committee. He also founded and served as Chairman of the St. Bernadette Community Carnival (Westlake, OH).

Nate lives in Westlake with his wife Rose; their two children: Jonathan (now a professional "skooter-rider" with over 40,000 followers on Instagram) and Nicole (an avid volleyball player, and "straight-A" student); and their dog "Cocoa." Nate has been an avid competitive runner since childhood and has also competed in Marathons, Triathlons & Adventure Races; but now primarily focuses on mountain-biking since 2014. He was born in Toronto, Canada, but became a U.S. Citizen in 1987.

Appendix 2

About the Editor: James Mayer

James Mayer ("Jim") graduated from Xavier University (OH) (A.B., 1966), and from Case Western Reserve School of Law (J.D., 1969).

His professional career has included general and corporate law practice in the Cleveland, Ohio area, and currently specialized services for the legal profession.

Jim and his wife Susan

He is a grateful member of Alcoholics Anonymous and is active in recovery circles. Jim and his lovely wife, Susan, reside in Avon Lake, Ohio, and enjoy spending time with their loving children and grandchildren.

Author's Note: I am truly grateful to Jim for not only serving as my inspirational sponsor in the AA Program and for his genuine friendship, but for the incredible and time-consuming work he put forth on this book project while serving as editor.

Thank you, Jim, for your kindness, and for the countless hours you put into helping me shape the many important messages contained herein, that will hopefully help others, one day at a time.

Appendix 3

About "Foreward" Author: Pastor Konan Stephens

Konan Stephens currently serves as the Lead Pastor for C3 Church in Columbus, Ohio, which he founded in 2006. He also serves as the Founder and President of the C3 Network, which has planted 30 new churches both in the US and across the world with a vision of planting hundreds more.

In his role as Pastor, Konan serves as a motivational speaker to constantly challenge people to reach higher. Through his amazing feats of endurance and perseverance, he shares his personal experiences of how to push past his own personal limitations in order to succeed, and constantly challenges others to "live their adventure" by pushing beyond their personal limitations. Whether it is climbing a mountain, running an ultra-marathon or mountain biking the Tour Divide, he leads by example to "live life to the fullest."

Prior to joining C3 Church in 2006, Konan was State Youth Director of the Ohio Ministry Network of the Assemblies of God from January 2000 through August 2006; and served as Youth Pastor for the Harbor of Hope Assembly of God, from 1996 through 2000. Konan obtained his formal education from the International Bible College Seminary, Pastoral Ministries from 1997 through 1998; attended Southern University from 1995 through 1996; and Malone College from 1993 through 1995.

Konan is married to his wife Jennifer and enjoys life with their amazing children.

Appendix 4*

The Twelve Steps of Alcoholics Anonymous.
(* Source: Hazelden Betty Ford Foundation: https://hazeldenbettyford.org)

Addiction is not a choice. That statement may not seem groundbreaking today, but the idea of alcoholism as an illness was a new concept in 1939 when the book *Alcoholics Anonymous: The Story of How More Than One Hundred Men Have Recovered from Alcoholism* was published.

Known as the *Big Book of Alcoholics Anonymous*, the publication not only changed the conversation about alcoholism, but also catapulted the Twelve Step model of recovery into the public's eye. Today, Narcotics Anonymous, Cocaine Anonymous, Heroin Anonymous, Gamblers Anonymous, Sexaholics Anonymous and Food Addicts in Recovery Anonymous all offer a Twelve Step approach to recovery based on the success of the original AA model.

The Twelve Steps were adopted nearly word-for-word by Al-Anon/Alateen, a program of recovery for the families and friends affected by a loved one's drinking (whether or not the alcoholic recognizes they have a drinking problem).

What Are the Twelve Steps of Alcoholics Anonymous?
The Twelve Steps are a set of guiding principles in addiction treatment that outline a course of action for tackling problems including alcoholism, drug addiction and compulsion.

Step 1: We admitted we were powerless over alcohol -- that our lives had become unmanageable.

Step 2: Came to believe that a Power greater than ourselves could restore us to sanity.

Step 3: Made a decision to turn our will and our lives over to the care of God *as we understood Him.*

Step 4: Made a searching and fearless moral inventory of ourselves.

Step 5: Admitted to God, to ourselves and to another human being the exact nature of our wrongs.

Step 6: Were entirely ready to have God remove all these defects of character.

Step 7: Humbly asked Him to remove our shortcomings.

Step 8: Made a list of all persons we had harmed and became willing to make amends to them all.

Step 9: Made direct amends to such people wherever possible, except when to do so would injure them or others.

Step 10: Continued to take personal inventory and when we were wrong promptly admitted it.

Step 11: Sought through prayer and meditation to improve our conscious contact with God *as we understood Him*, praying only for knowledge of His will for us and the power to carry that out.

Step 12: Having had a spiritual awakening as the result of these Steps, we tried to carry this message to alcoholics, and to practice these principles in all our affairs.

Where Did the Twelve Steps Originate? Bill Wilson and Dr. Bob Smith, the two men behind AA, drew their inspiration for the Twelve Steps from the Oxford Group who advocated that all problems rooted in fear and selfishness could be changed through the power of God by following the "Four Absolutes," a moral inventory of "absolute honesty, purity, unselfishness and love," and through public sharing/confession. The Oxford Group also believed in the work of American psychologist William James, particularly his philosophy of pragmatism and "The Will to Believe" doctrine (by changing the inner attitudes of the mind, we can change the outer aspect of life), and William Silkworth, MD, one of the first medical professionals to characterize alcoholism as a disease.

When AA was founded in 1935 by Bill W. and Dr. Bob as a fellowship of alcoholics working together to overcome their drinking problems, the 12-Steps acted as a set of guidelines for spiritual and character development—a blueprint for recovery. The Twelve Steps serve the same purpose today. As described by Alcoholics Anonymous, following these guidelines "as a way of life, can expel the obsession to drink and enable the sufferer to become happily and usefully whole."

What's the Purpose of the Twelve Steps? The purpose is to recover from compulsive, out-of-control addictive behaviors and restore manageability and order to your life. It is a way of seeing that your behavior is only a symptom, a sort of "check engine" light to discovering what is really going on under the hood.

How and Why Does it Work? According to the American Society of Addiction Medicine, "Twelve Step facilitation therapy is a tried-and-true proven approach." (There's a reason, after all, why people still "work the Steps" more than 80 years later.) **How does it work?** People are encouraged to take an honest look at themselves, then deconstruct their egos and rebuild, little by little. **Why does it work?** The Steps encourage the practice of honesty, humility, acceptance, courage, compassion, forgiveness and self-discipline: pathways to positive behavioral change, emotional well-being and spiritual growth.

What Are the Twelve Traditions? The Twelve Traditions are associated with the 12-Steps, only rather than personal guidelines for the addict or alcoholic, they are general guidelines for healthy relationships between the group members and other groups. According to AA, "By 1946, it had become possible to draw sound conclusions about the kinds of attitude, practice and function that would best suit AA's purpose. Those principles, which had emerged from strenuous group experience, were codified by Bill in what today are the Twelve Traditions of Alcoholics Anonymous. A successful formula for AA unity and functioning had been achieved and put into practice."

Do You Have to be Religious in Order to Follow the Twelve Steps? No. While it is true that the 12-Steps were originally based on the principles of a spiritual organization, the world is not the same as it was in 1935 when AA and the 12-Step Program was founded. The word "God" was eventually replaced with "Higher Power" to be more accessible to everyone, regardless of faith traditions or beliefs. A Higher Power doesn't have to be God; it could be nature, the universe, fate, karma, your support system, the recovery group itself, medical professionals or whatever you feel is outside of and greater than yourself/your ego. What you believe to be a Higher Power is a very personal thing.

In Step One: What Does it Mean to "Admit Powerlessness?" Admitting powerlessness is not the same as admitting weakness. It means asking for help, leaning on others and relying on your support system. It means admitting and accepting that you are living with a disease that alters your brain. It might seem backward, but when you can admit that you do not have power, you can access the power you need.

How Long Does It Take for the Twelve Steps to Work? With the Twelve Steps, there is no hard and fast timeline. The Steps are meant to be addressed in sequential order, but there is no one "right" way to approach them. Sometimes people need a break between Steps, sometimes people need to spend longer on one step than another, some people never stop working the 12-Steps because they become part of life.

Pros of the Twelve Steps
- The Twelve Steps are widely known, established and organized (it is one of the oldest programs around).
- Those struggling with substance abuse have access to a supportive network of peers.
- It is easy to find a meeting where the Twelve Steps are practiced.
- There is little to no cost to those in need -- it is a free intervention to address a chronic disease.

Cons of the Twelve Steps
- Some people are not interested in participating in group settings.
- Due to the anonymous nature of the group, there is a lack of official shared success rates.
- The Steps are criticized for not addressing the needs of those struggling with mental illness.
- When the Twelve Steps were originally created, science had yet to prove a genetic link to addiction.

What does "working the 12-Steps" mean?
As you begin to hear people talk about "working" the steps, you may wonder, "What does that even mean?" Simply put, it is working with a fellow addict or alcoholic to better yourself.

What Are Some Alternatives to a 12-Step Program? The Substance Abuse and Mental Health Services Administration (*SAMHSA*) identifies many national groups that offer an alternative approach to the Twelve Steps. These groups are secular in nature, emphasize internal control, evolve with changing research in the field of addiction and generally oppose labels that define past behavior.

The SAMHSA list includes some of the following:

Self-Management and Recovery Training (SMART Recovery): Emphasis on learning how to cope with urges and cravings, based on cognitive behavioral therapy and motivational interviewing.

Secular Organizations for Sobriety (SOS): Develop strategies to achieve and maintain sobriety (abstinence) from alcohol and drug addiction, food addiction, etc.

Moderation Management: Designed for those who think their drinking has become a problem and they want to moderate it before it gets out of control. Focus on 30 days of abstinence and guidelines about moderate drinking.

Local Cleveland (OH) Based Groups
2-CIRCLE Racing is partnering with:

Lean-In Recovery Center: 20033 Detroit Road, Rocky River, OH 44116. Phone: 216.387.6072. An emotionally protected, clinically informed residential center that is a collaborative experience to help residents gain long term sustainable recovery habits steeped in the 12-Steps.

Rebel Rising Wellness: 20525 Center Ridge Rd, Suite 615. Rocky River, OH 44116. Phone: 216.385.8050. A private individual therapy center and sober active community for women; focused on counseling, coaching and recovery.

Everything Recovery: 3300 Wooster Road, Rocky River, OH 44116. Phone: (216) 772-2075. A community center that provides programming to celebrate victory over substance use disorder by reinforcing positive choices through seminars, fellowship, family and peer support, and entertainment.

APPENDIX 5

THE AA PROMISES

What do the AA promises mean?
The **AA Promises** are **meant** to be a promise experienced in recovery. In sum, they are statements that summarize outcomes that will likely result by thoroughly working the 12-Step Program. The time frame in which they come to fruition is different for each person.

As experienced on numerous occasions throughout my Great Divide ride, many of the "promises" illustrated below did indeed occur, and I have also experienced many of these same promises during my four-years of sobriety. *They do come true.*

Here are the promises, as outlined in the *Big Book of Alcoholics Anonymous*, and are *what we strive for*:

1. If we are painstaking about this phase of our development, we will be amazed before we are halfway through.

2. We are going to know a new freedom and a new happiness.

3. We will not regret the past nor wish to shut the door on it.

4. We will comprehend the word serenity and we will know peace.

5. No matter how far down the scale we have gone, we will see how our experience can benefit others.

6. That feeling of uselessness and self-pity will disappear.

7. We will lose interest in selfish things and gain interest in our fellows.

8. Self-seeking will slip away.

9. Our whole attitude and outlook upon life will change.

10. Fear of people and of economic insecurity will leave us.

11. We will intuitively know how to handle situations which used to baffle us.

12. We will suddenly realize that God is doing for us what we could not do for ourselves.

Are these extravagant promises? We think not.

They are being fulfilled among us: sometimes quickly, sometimes slowly. They will always materialize if we work for them.

Appendix 6

Great Divide Bike-Packing List

My Great Divide ride was self-supported, which means that everything needed was packed on my bike. Here is a list of the items I brought with me and where they fit on my bike:

Bags for Bike

Frame	Revelate Frame Bag	For food & water
Top Tube	Specialized Top Tube Bag	For phone & electronics
Top Tube/Seat	Specialzied Triangular	For cords & batteries
Handlebar	Revelate water bottle & feed bag (2)	For bear spray & water bottles
Rear Seat Clothing Bag	Specialized Burra-Burr Stabilizer Seatpack 10	For clothing
Compression Bag	E-vent Waterproof (3)	For sleeping bag, tent & air mattress

Sleep System

Sleeping Bag	Marmot 30 degree	Left Fork Bag
Tent	Survival Frog 1-Person	Right Fork Bag
Sleep Pad	ThermoRest NeoAir	Under AeroBar

Clothing

Bib top (1)	BeFreeRideBikes.com	Rear Seat Bag
Bib shorts (2)	BeFreeRideBikes.com	Rear Seat Bag
Long sleeve jersey	BeFreeRideBikes.com	Rear Seat Bag
Baselayer	Under Armour	Rear Seat Bag
Wool Top	Smartwool long sleeve	Rear Seat Bag
Riding gloves	Pearl Izumi	Rear Seat Bag
Wool gloves	Giro smart wool	Rear Seat Bag
Winter gloves	Specialized Gore Windstopper	Rear Seat Bag
Leg Warmers	Specialized	Rear Seat Bag
Socks (3)	Smart wool, waterproof & compression	Rear Seat Bag
Sunglasses	Drug Mart $7.99 Special	Rear Seat Bag
Skull cap	Headsweats	Rear Seat Bag
Rain-jacket	ShowersPass Elite 2.1	Rear Seat Bag
Rain-pants	Showers Pass	Rear Seat Bag
Wind vest	BeFreeRideBikes.com	Rear Seat Bag
Shoes	Specialized MTB	Worn all times

Water, Food & Survival

Spot Locator	Spot tracker	Monitored by Trackleaders.com
First Aid kit	Just the essentials	Frame bag
Water Bladder	Camelback	Frame Bag
I-Phone & earphones	Apple	Top tube bag
Batteries	Everyready lithium	Rear tube bag
Chamois cream	Chamois Butt'r	Frame bag
Toothbrush & paste	Crest	Top tube bag
Lip balm & sunscreen	Drug Mart	Top tube bag
Power bank, chargers & recharge cords	Per each device	Rear tube bag
Water Filters	Sawyer mini filter (2)	Frame bag

Repair, Bike Parts & Essentials

Inner tubes (2)	Specialized	Frame bag
Multi-purpose tool	Crank Brothers	Tool can under frame
11-speed master chain link	Santa Cruz related	Tool can under frame
CO2 (air)	Bike shop bought (2)	Tool can under frame
Tire boots	Patches for tire (3)	Tool can under frame
Tire levers	Standard	Tool can under frame
Derailleur hangar	Santa Cruz	Tool can under frame
Cleat/bolts	Specialized	Tool can under frame
Rotor bolts	Santa Cruz fit	Tool can under frame
Pedals	Egg-Beaters	Newly installed
Supplies	Zip ties & duct tape	Frame bag
Supplies	Extra chain & lube	Tool can under frame
Supplies	Mini pump & spokes	Frame bag
Sanitizer wipes	Standard store bought	Frame bag
Helmet	Specialized	Worn all times
Spare brake pads	Shimano (2)	Tool can under frame

Lighting & Navigation

GPS	Garmin Etrex-30x	On handle-bars
Maps	Adventure Cycling	In frame bag
Front Lighting	Lezyme	On aero-bars
Rear Lighting	Lezyme	On rear seat bag

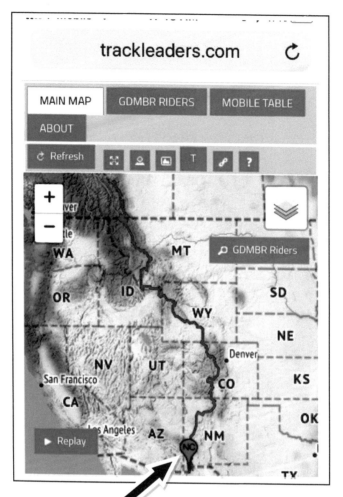

Victory! This is my satellite "dot" that charted my progress along the way.

As you can see, I made it to Mexico!!!

To view <u>Nate's Video Diary</u> of his <u>Great Divide Ride</u> including *his infamous dance routine* at the finish...
*Go to **youtube** and search for:*
Nates 2020 Ride

A Final Thought…